Kevin Callan

Published by Kevin Callan Books 2019
Copyright © 2019 Kevin Callan Books
Text copyright © 2019 Kevin Callan

All rights reserved. No part of this publication may be reproduced, stored in a retrieval system, or transmitted in any former by any means, electronic, mechanical, photocopying, recording or otherwise, without the prior written permission of the publisher/author.

First printing

Published by:
Kevin Callan Books
805 Simcoe St.
Bridgenorth, ON
K0L 1H0
callan@sympatico.ca

kevincallan.com

Cover and interior design: Gillian Stead
Edited by: Kaydi Pyette

Thanks to all the Algonquin Provincial Park staff, volunteers, campers and canoeists who have protected and enhanced one of Canada's best wilderness treasures.

Contents

Route Map		10
Introduction	Finding My Happy Place	11
CHAPTER 1	No Country for Old Men	14
CHAPTER 2	My Love Affair with Algonquin	19
CHAPTER 3	It Begins	24
CHAPTER 4	The Big East — An Absolute Slog!	28
CHAPTER 5	The End Is Near	33
CHAPTER 6	Entering Algonquin — Finally!	38
CHAPTER 7	Hiding a Paddle	41
CHAPTER 8	Those Were the Days	44
CHAPTER 9	Always Say Hello	48

CHAPTER 10	Butt Lake Becomes Ralph Bice Lake — Thank Goodness	52
CHAPTER 11	A Bump in the Night	54
CHAPTER 12	Moose Pee on the Campsite	57
CHAPTER 13	Homesick on the Nipissing	64
CHAPTER 14	The Trojan Horse	69
CHAPTER 15	Stolen Whisky	73
CHAPTER 16	Breaking Park Rules	76
CHAPTER 17	History Along the Petawawa	79
CHAPTER 18	Bill Mason's River	82
CHAPTER 19	Trout on the Crow River	89
CHAPTER 20	A Toast to Swifty on Lake Lavielle	92
CHAPTER 21	Opeongo — Algonquin's Largest Lake	97
CHAPTER 22	Getting Comfortable	105
CHAPTER 23	Portage Etiquette	110
CHAPTER 24	Ingenious Nasty Beavers	113
CHAPTER 25	Bob Dylan Went to Camp	116
CHAPTER 26	Is Algonquin Too Dangerous for Kids?	122
CHAPTER 27	Civilization on the Horizon	126
CHAPTER 28	Down the Oxtongue	128
CHAPTER 29	You Shall Not Pass!	133
Epilogue		139
Tips Before You Go	Do We Have Enough Whisky?	141
About the Author		151

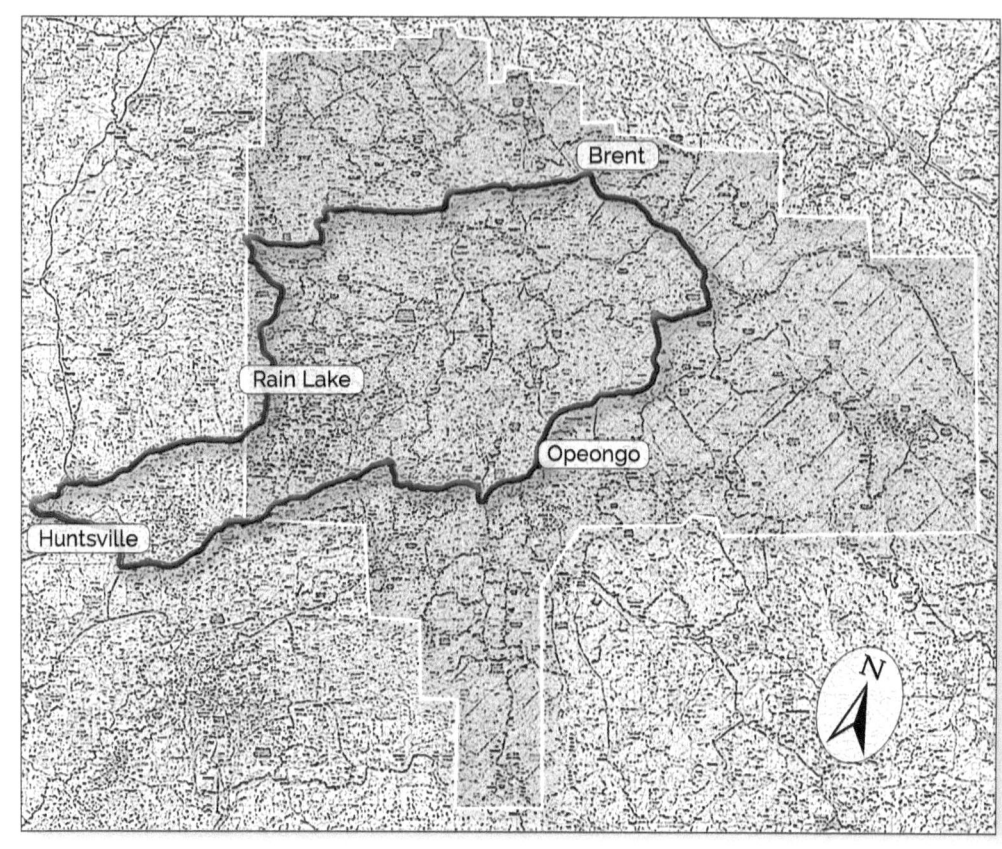

Algonquin Provincial Park's the Meanest Link showing the start and finish at Huntsville and each food drop off access point as the route travels clockwise in and out of the park boundary.

Once Around Algonquin

INTRODUCTION

Finding My Happy Place

"The wilderness is healing, a therapy for the soul."
NICHOLAS KRISTOF

I knew it was too good to be true. The plane flying me home was on time — early, in fact. The good-humored passengers, including myself, boarded in an orderly manner, everyone considerate of one another. Life was good, or at least the best it can get at a busy airport. I was headed home after spending a weekend presenting at Canoecopia, North America's largest paddling event, held in Madison, Wisconsin. It can best be likened to a Star Trek convention for canoeists.

After a promising taxi out to the runway, things changed. The revving engine dropped to a faint hum and the brakes beneath us squeaked as we slowed. The pilot announced there was a delay and we would have to sit patiently on the tarmac until we got the go-ahead to take-off.

As 10 minutes stretched into an hour-and-a-half wait, the same friendly people I'd boarded with became barbaric, complaining and cursing the airline. The guy beside me smelled terrible — a foul mix of body odor, foot odor, bad breath and something unidentifiable. I felt claustrophobic.

Sleep was impossible. I read a magazine back to back, three times, as the battery for my iPod drained to nothing.

To survive, I needed to go to my happy place. I searched my bag for entertainment and found an old Algonquin Provincial Park map folded up at the bottom. It was weathered, stained with coffee, and even had a few unlucky mosquitoes squashed on it. Planning my next canoe trip in Algonquin became my salvation. By the time we touched down in Toronto, I had a plan to paddle a 20-day, 350-kilometer (217-mile) loop around the park. The epic route is called the Meanest Link.

The route was named in honor and memory of Bill Swift Sr., one of the founders of Algonquin Outfitters. At first, I thought the route was named for Bill Swift's character. Swifty, as he was often called, had other nicknames, such as Mean Dude and Meanest, a tribute to his gruff persona. However, the more I looked at the details of the trip, the more it appeared the route is named appropriately. It's one mean trip.

The route crosses some of the park's largest lakes, and travels six of its rivers — three of which have to be navigated upstream. There are 93 portages, ranging from 50 meters (54 yards) to five kilometers (3.1 miles). The total portage distance adds up to 68 kilometers (42 miles). And that's with a single carry; I usually portage my gear in two loads, multiplying the distance I walk by three. Yikes! A one-carry portage would mean bringing only the essential equipment and no luxury items. No camp chairs, puffy pillows, and definitely not an unlimited supply of spirits.

The journey is the brainchild of Algonquin Outfitters staffers, Alex Hurley and Gord Baker, who dreamed up the ambitious paddle during the summer of 2004.

Gord and Alex combined four challenging canoe routes, connecting the four distant Algonquin Outfitters stores serving Algonquin. The store in the town of Huntsville and the one on Oxtongue Lake are situated just outside the park's southwestern border. Another store is on Lake Opeongo in the southeast and the final one is on Cedar Lake, in the far northeast corner of the park.

The rules to complete the Meanest Link are lengthy but straightforward. Paddlers can start the loop at any store and travel in either direction. You can do a section at a time or the whole loop in one go, which is known as the Full Link. No solo trips are recognized for safety reasons. You have to use the same watercraft for the whole section. You can paddle as fast or as slow as you like. The Meanest Link is not a race, but it's perceived as one by most. You must visit, and preferably stay on, Bill Swift's favorite site on Lake Lavielle, and cheers a preferred beverage — his was a can of Genesee Cream Ale. And on the Opeongo to Oxtongue Link, you have to go up the Little Mad to Source Lake, stop at Camp Pathfinder to pay your respects to the spot where it all began for Bill Swift in Algonquin.

I had no intention of following all the rules. Not that I'm one to defy tradition, but my reasoning behind this trip had little to do with completing a marathon-style competition. I just wanted to complete a full jaunt around one of my favorite places to go on a canoe trip. I was also on a mission of sorts. I had two paddles to hide along the way for a scavenger hunt master-minded by some volunteers on social media to get more people paddling. I figured if I spent some quality time in Algonquin, hid a couple of paddles along the way to encourage others to get out more, and maybe even cheated a little bit here and there, I'd have an incredible journey.

I asked my regular canoe mate, Andy Baxter, to accompany me. He's a good friend, an accomplished paddler, strong as a bull on portages, and he's paddled countless trips with me. He also has the comedic flair of legendary Red Skelton. Poor Andy blindly agreed to come along on the trip, not requesting any of the details in advance.

We're not the typical candidates to paddle the Meanest Link — it's more popular amongst the type A crowd; those who strive for perfection and personal challenge. Our reasons for attempting it were a desire for adventure, to soak up solitude, and to spend as much time as possible out in the woods. That's what draws me to wilderness areas — not to survive but to thrive, to comfortably take in it all in for as long as possible. The record for completing the loop was seven-and-a-half days — we allocated three weeks.

Andy and I are turtles, not hares.

1
No Country for Old Men

"Maybe it's true that life begins at 50.
But everything else starts to wear out, fall out, or spread out."
PHYLLIS DILLER

Andy and I had both recently turned 50. The milestone was not my primary reason for an ambitious trip like the Meanest Link, but one day I found myself offering details of my first colonoscopy to complete strangers and it gave me a new perspective. I'm not getting any younger. It made sense to do the Meanest Link now.

I don't consider 50 old, but I'm long enough in the tooth to be adding things to the bucket list I started many years ago.

As a boy, I wanted to skim a perfect stone, Tarzan on a rope swing, discover dinosaur bones, light a fire without matches, and paddle a canoe.

In high school, I added wilder things to the bucket, like playing the drums, seeing KISS in concert, skinny-dipping, getting past first base, and canoeing down a wild river.

As a young man, I wanted to work a job where I was outdoors more than indoors. I wanted to save wilderness, get past third base, and canoe down an even wilder river.

The thing about buckets is you put a whole bunch of things in them and then forget about it for a while. If you're lucky, as you go you get to cross off a bunch of stuff. I've done most of those early things, and even more I never would have thought to include.

I've paddled Bill Mason's canoe. I've portaged across the front lawn at Parliament Hill and was forced off by the RCMP for having a "vessel of too much magnitude." I've chatted with great musicians Gord Downie of The Tragically Hip, Jim Cuddy of Blue Rodeo, Grapes of Wrath's Kevin Kane, and Jann Arden, all about the simplicity of canoe tripping. I've chewed the fat with legendary scribblers like Farley Mowat, James Raffan, Margaret Atwood, Pierre Berton, Roy MacGregor and Red Green.

Early in my adult life I became a published author. I beam with joy every time someone asks me what I do for a living. The best part of being a writer is I get to spend more than 60 nights a year sleeping in a tent.

My life seems fulfilling — and it is — but my imagination is again filling the bucket for things I want to accomplish before reaching my Golden Girls era.

I'm not talking about the customary bucket-list places to paddle like the Nahanni. And my dreams are not necessarily places I've never paddled before. Sure, I'd add to the list of bodies of water such as the Florida Everglades, Great Slave Lake, or the Winisk or Moisie rivers in a heartbeat. But my priority is to revisit life-long favorites in my home province of Ontario. I want to return to Woodland Caribou's Artery Lake, the upper stretch of Missinaibi River, Killarney's Great Mountain Lake, and the northern shore of Lake Nipigon.

I'd also love to return to wilderness hermitages like Wendell Beckwith's place in wild Wabakimi or Jimmy McOuat's White Otter Castle on the Turtle River. It would be awesome to savor a famous Sourtoe Cocktail in Dawson City after a Yukon River trip, and I'd like to organize a whisky tour in Ireland, similar to the canoe trip I did on the Spey River in Scotland.

However, circumnavigating Algonquin is higher on my bucket list than all of these.

I'd also like to build a canoe and ink a portage sign on my chest, forearm or maybe my buttock. I've always wanted to carve a wooden spoon, go solo for more than two months, play the penny whistle around the campfire, sit amongst a pack of wolves and howl with them, catch a brook trout with a homemade fly, and have a cup of tea with the highest-ranked First Nations elder to thank them for sharing the best mode of transport to navigate these wild areas.

Last but not least — and I'll have you know that I did make it past first base a time or two — I regret never yet making love in a canoe. While I can't imagine the actual physical act being all that comfortable, I think the actualizing of Pierre Berton's definition of what it takes to be a true Canadian makes perfect sense as a bucket-list item.

The canoe is a quintessentially Canadian icon. Doin' it in a voluminous jacuzzi in central Ontario's posh cottage country would be interesting. Making out in a hay field in the middle of prairie Saskatchewan, or in a king-size bed at the Chateau Frontenac overlooking the cobbled streets of old Quebec City would be impressive. But none of them are as Canadian or as high on my bucket list as making love in a canoe.

Being over the 50-year hump doesn't feel old — until a younger person reminds you of it. There's no need to buy into that thinking though, right?

Alex Traynor and Noah Booth are boyish video bloggers who call themselves the Northern Scavengers, and who completed the Meanest Link in just nine days in 2018. I loaned these two young adventurers one of my canoes for a different big trip in the far north, insisting they take one of my lightweight and durable Prospectors rather than their sinkable, flat-bottomed scow. They couldn't thank me enough, and I think they revered me as some kind of Jedi of the canoeing world. They even called me Uncle Kev, as in, "Thanks for the canoe, Uncle Kev." That was awkward.

I get it. I'm not far away from getting a senior's discount at the pharmacy. I've been writing and making presentations at shows for well over 30 years. Traynor and Booth are 26 years old. My first book came out the year they were born. I've made a career of trying to convince others to get outside and paddle for more than three decades now. Sometimes I feel like I've seen it all.

I can remember running rapids without wearing a helmet. I know the feeling of a cold butt on the seat of a Grumman. I was a member of a canoe club that wouldn't allow kayakers to join. I attended the grand opening of the Canadian Canoe Museum. I remember the early Old Town ads introducing a revolutionary new material called Royalex.

I cried the day Bill Mason died.

I've lived through the era of the movie *Deliverance* inspiring new paddlers to get on rivers, and witnessed social media forums that have the word "paddle" in the title but are all about the porn industry instead.

I've watched the cult-like fervor for paddling books fizzle. I've seen canoe movies go from Beta and VHS to DVDs to YouTube. I got excited once filming a documentary in Quetico Provincial Park with a state-of-the-art high definition camera. Not long ago, I helped film a documentary in Nova Scotia with a 360-degree virtual reality camera.

I've loaded 35mm film into the backs of cameras and used Dan Gibson's nature sounds while editing actual movie film instead of downloading digitally mastered loon calls served up by Google.

My first book was written on a typewriter. My second book was saved on a floppy disk. My last one was typed on a computer, saved digitally and uploaded to the Cloud — not one word scribbled on paper.

I showed trays of slides during presentations. I learned PowerPoint. Now I just Bluetooth my presentations from my phone — imagine saying that to an A/V guy in the '80s! Radio shows have turned into podcasts. And these days, I do more live streaming on Facebook than face-to-face interviews on television morning shows.

Through all of this, I've listened over the years to crusty, bearded, Tilley-capped men in plaid proclaiming, "Canoeing is dead." They mailed me letters. Then emails. Now I receive these doomsday decrees through Facebook Messenger. They write to tell me kayaks and stand up paddleboards will rule the world. They say canoeists will just fade away.

Take it from an aging canoeist who's been around the bend on a lot of rivers, they're wrong. Canoe sales have increased 110 percent since 2016. Since 2014, canoeing participation has increased by 40 percent, especially among young families and Millennials.

Take, for example, the Northern Scavengers. Here are two guys the same age I was when I launched my first book. They're creating a community, using the technological tools of today, where campers of all levels can come to give or gain a little insight on anything backcountry related. On their website, they've written: "The best way to appreciate the raw beauty is to immerse yourself in it. Camping is an unparalleled physical journey that can connect us to the land in the most organic way and can bring us to places unbothered by the modern world."

Though Bill Mason died the year before my first book and a year before the Northern Scavengers where born, the boys have this Mason quote on their About Us page: "The canoe feels very much alive, alive with the life of the river."

Canoeing will never die.

2
My Love Affair with Algonquin

"Algonquin Park, so wild and free,
You've got a lariat on me,
Its forest aisles and temples grand,
Immortal shrines, not made by hand.
Oh, Mother Nature, hold my hand,
And guide me thru this mystic land,
And let me know and understand,
Why this paradise was planned.

On rugged hills, the towering pines,
Nod in the fragrant ozone winds,
Bearing pine-laden zephyrs of health,
To cheeks that wore the shade of death.
Algonquin's lakes and rippling streams,
Haven of rest and soothing dreams,
On this the Master stamped his brand,
And christened it, God's fairy-land."

JOHN W. MILLAR (1927),
poet and Algonquin Provincial Park superintendent

As an author of several canoeing guidebooks, I spend a good portion of my life telling paddlers where to go. So, you might think I have a good answer to the most common question I am asked: "Kevin, where's your favorite place to paddle?"

The answer is not as easy as you might think.

I've been to many wild places and have fond memories from each and every trip. Each route is special — some are spectacularly scenic, others very remote. Some offer something entirely unique, like wild fishing, incredible wildlife watching or breathtaking campsites.

When someone asks me about my favorite route, I often rattle off a couple of favorite routes in Algonquin or Killarney Provincial Park. Then I mention some lesser-known provincial parks and wilderness areas — Quetico, Woodland Caribou and Wabakimi. From there I ramble on about lost routes only the die-hards have heard of — Kirkpatrick, Chiniguichi, Tatachikapika. But why stick close to home? My growing list soon includes western rivers, like the Milk or the Bowron Lakes chain. And don't forget about the East, I tell them.

Before long, I've mentioned far-off trips to the Scottish Highlands and the inland rivers of Ireland, and the person who asked the question has long since regretted saying anything at all.

I once delivered a presentation about the best North American canoe routes at an outdoor show in the United States. In the front row, a paddler — wearing the standard Tilley hat and holding a pen and paper at the ready — looked hungry for answers. "So, Kevin," he asked me during the Q&A, "which is your favorite canoe route?"

Inspired by his Tilley hat free of a single stain or squashed mosquito, I responded by rhyming off a litany of pre-loved routes. It was the wrong approach.

"It's the next one I'm going on," I told him, elusive and sly. "And after that, my favorite will be the next one."

I hoped my clever response would inspire the man to paddle out and discover his own wilderness route — and maybe even get his Tilley hat a bit dirty.

Instead, the man stared blankly at me.

"But Algonquin is always a good choice," I stammered. "Next question!"

Algonquin is my go-to. It's familiar wilderness to me. I've been exploring there since I was in diapers. It's where I start my paddling season every year, and where I end it, too.

There's much to be said about paddling a familiar place. It doesn't offer the same feeling as traveling to places unknown does and yet, it can still surprise you.

Exploring a new place expands horizons, and it's why I started canoe tripping in the first place. Unfolding a new map, scouting rapids, locating portages, searching for feasible campsites, dreaming of magnificent grandeur around the next bend in the river — that's at the heart of canoe tripping.

That same impulse fueled explorers and voyageurs to set out into the unknown, venture to the edges of the map and fill in a few details along the way.

Deepening my understanding of a place I already know and love is why I really wanted to paddle Algonquin's Meanest Link.

I've done some extensive trips in the park but nothing like an entire trip around it. Once I started planning, gathering maps and packing gear, I began to second-guess the route. And I was right to rethink it. It's one crazy trip. Only a handful of paddlers had completed the full loop, and all were in far better shape than me. What kept me going was the pure pleasure of spending quality time in the sheer magnitude of Algonquin. This is one big and beautiful park.

I have to admit, there are times I question going to Algonquin. The average portage in the park is well over a kilometer, so portaging becomes commonplace. The park can also be crowded in summer and the odd disrespectful person who trashes campsites and lacks proper camp etiquette inevitably shows up. The most accessible places in the park are along the Highway 60 corridor, and those can seem a little zoo-like with human-habituated wildlife and several campgrounds boasting a combined 1,200 drive-in sites.

The good far outweighs those minor negatives though, and that's what has kept me coming back, year after year. I have memories aplenty. Spring canoe trips in search of trophy-sized trout; fall backpacking trips with the forest lit up with changing colors; pulling a toboggan full of winter gear across a frozen lake, where the sense of isolation is so great I feel like the only man on Earth; and even pitching a tent in a busy campground and camping beside complete strangers, who quickly become friends for life.

Algonquin offers all that, and more, to more than a million people each year. It has enough wilderness to satisfy the soul while inspiring many of us to search for even wilder places beyond its borders. Long portages and crowded campgrounds be damned — I love Algonquin, and always will.

It was tourists who initially helped protect Algonquin. Devoted anglers, renowned artists and wealthy vacationers arrived by train and stayed at lavish hotels. Many were outdoorsy Canadians, but more than 30 percent were from south of the border or Europe. They were all drawn to Algonquin for a good reason. Algonquin Park provides some of Canada's best canoeing, with over 2,400 lakes and 1,200 kilometers (745 miles) of streams and rivers located within the park, together forming a 2,000-kilometer-long (1,200 mile) interconnected system of canoe routes.

Tourists loved it here and grew concerned over the encroachment of agriculture and depleting fish and game. The dream was to protect the half-dozen watersheds that gave birth to the main rivers that flushed out of their familiar piece of paradise, and they succeeded. Algonquin Park was formed in 1893.

At the time, it was considered the most significant wilderness park in all of Canada — a place twice the size of the province of Prince Edward Island, or the size of the U.S. states of Delaware and Rhode Island combined. Algonquin is a quarter of the size of Belgium. It was promoted as the largest tract of dedicated bush in the world.

Since its creation, Algonquin has more than doubled in size, from 3,797 square kilometers (2,359 square miles) to 7,630 square kilometers (4,741 square miles). It's changed its name from Algonquin National Park to Algonquin Provincial Park (becoming Ontario's first provincial park) and expanded its borders eight times. Along the way, the original intent hasn't changed much. Park commissioners set out a plan well over 100 years ago to maintain watersheds, protect and encourage the growth of birds and animals, maintain the Park in a state of nature, do field experiments in systematic forestry to a limited scale, secure a place for healthy recreation, and to study the beneficial effects on the protection of a large forested area.

The popularity of Algonquin has continued to grow since its creation. People worship this place. The devotion of its fans give to the park far exceeds the loyalty others would give to their favorite rock band, hockey team, and even lover. Songs have been written (including three by The Tragically Hip), art created (the Group of Seven, Robert Bateman and Bill Mason, to name a few), books published (including from the legendary Roy MacGregor and Ralph Bice), as well as poems scribbled, theater performed, films produced, a symphony established, clubs gathered, and websites launched. Algonquin Park is world renowned. If you mention any other larger and wilder place in Canada, you surely won't get the same response, the same fidelity that Algonquinites give to their park.

Simply put, this remnant piece of semi-wilderness, a mere two-hour drive from Toronto's international airport, wouldn't be here if so many people didn't love it. They protected this large chunk of green amongst an ocean of development. The forest was managed, wildlife monitored, poachers arrested, and its solace shared by countless outdoor enthusiasts alike.

3
It Begins

"Twenty years from now you will be more disappointed by the things you didn't do than by the ones you did do. So throw off the bowlines, sail away from the safe harbor. Catch the trade winds in your sails. Explore. Dream. Discover."

MARK TWAIN

Bugs love the smell of a clean camper. Andy and I were fresh as it comes, smelling of shampoo and deodorant. Like pre-teens to a pop star, the black flies and mosquitoes flocked to us the moment we exited the vehicle.

We had stopped at Algonquin Outfitters on Oxtongue Lake to visit one of the Meanest Link founders, Gord Baker. We knew after a few days of paddling and portaging we would gather enough distasteful body odor to quell the bugs a bit. Already worried about the route ahead, the ravenous black flies didn't help our anxiety levels. To make matters worse, we met a father and son team who had just abandoned the Meanest Link route only a couple of days into their trip.

The father rushed across the parking lot to greet us, looking flustered. The son staggered behind. He had broken his toe at the end of day two while wading up the Big East River. The duo was helped out of the park by Gord and his staff. This was the father's third attempt at the Meanest Link, he told us. The year before, the son's twin brother had joined them, then bailed not far into the trip. Andy and I were starting to wonder what we'd gotten ourselves into.

It was mid-morning by the time we obtained our park permit, drove to the starting point at the town docks of Huntsville and found a safe place to leave the vehicle. There was no solid reasoning behind choosing to start at the Huntsville access point. But there was a specific rationale for going clockwise around the loop. It meant we'd have to paddle against the current on the Big East River as well as the Crow River, and a small stretch of the Madawaska River. However, Andy and I would be able to go with the current on the Nipissing River, which is the longest stretch of fast current on the route, as well as the swift-moving Petawawa and Oxtongue rivers.

A small gathering of staff from the Huntsville Algonquin Outfitters store came to wish us good luck and snap some photos. A local resident of the town also wandered over to warn us of what may lay ahead on the Big East River. The river and town had suffered a massive flood just a month before, and no one was quite sure what obstacles were waiting for us upstream.

Andy and I snubbed the local's warnings until we paddled away from the dock, paddled across Lake Vernon, reached the mouth of the Big East River, and then began our paddle against the current by maneuvering around a half-submerged stove, refrigerator, barbecue, lawnmower and a complete woodshed. The flood had done some serious damage.

The flood was brought on by melting snow and an abundance of rain — 50 millimeters (three inches) in a 24-hour period. It was a record high water level for Huntsville and the town declared a state of emergency. Roads were washed out, bridges destroyed, and 150 people removed from 70 homes.

By looking at the river delta, I could tell it wasn't the first time the Big East had flooded. The mounds of sediment flushed downriver, into Lake Vernon, have built up over the years. The action has created an ecological masterpiece. The delta is an absolute oasis, giving home to a rare deciduous swamp forest, made up of red and silver maple, birch and ash.

The first stretch of the Big East is a stunning ribbon of blue, made up of deep, slow-moving water. The banks are sandy bluffs, topped with dense forest. It makes sense why the Natives, who once traveled the river, called it Wabun Login — or Sand River.

At first, a few cottages dotted the shoreline and bridges crossed the river, including the one for busy Highway 11. This area is the most popular section to paddle. The lower portion of the Big East makes for a perfect weekend camp out, especially for the local teenagers looking for a place to drink beer and smoke dope. Andy and I stopped for our first lunch break on a sandbar and discovered some empty beer cans and a stack of nudie mags — *Hustlers* and *Playboys* from the '90s — stored under some cooking pots beside a campfire ring. Don't horny teens have the Internet nowadays?

As the river winds its way towards Arrowhead Provincial Park, it becomes too shallow for motorboats, even Jet Skis. The shoreline is protected by a newly developed waterway park. There are countless oxbows, twisting the river around impressive sand cliffs. One, in particular, is named the Big Bend and rises 35 meters up from the river and provides a popular lookout.

Just past Arrowhead Provincial Park, we decided to end our first day, and chose one of the many sandbars to make camp. I pitched the tent back in a cedar grove while Andy worked on building up a fire pit on the exposed beach front. It was a good stop for the day, especially our first day. Dinner was steak and salad. Having a non-dehydrated meal the first night out is a ritual for us. After pouring the post-meal dram of whisky in our tin cups, we sat by the campfire and soaked it all in. We were alone now and truly enjoying our wilderness solitude. It reminded me of a quote I like from Robert Perkins' film, *One Man in a Boat*. Perkins looks out at a remote wilderness section and says, "I feel like rolling it up in a ball and swallowing it, so no one else can have it."

Around midnight, we woke up to a male whitetail deer snorting, whistling and kicking the dirt directly outside our tent. We had pitched our camp right on its run, and it wasn't pleased about it. That's what you get for paddling a route rarely traveled.

Andy drew the figurative short straw and crawled out of the tent to let the buck know we weren't up for moving camp. He also took the opportunity to take a pee. Unfortunately, the mosquitoes had gathered in insane numbers just outside our tent door, waiting for a feast. Poor Andy crawled back in the tent and into his sleeping bag itching and scratching his groin. Then, a crash of thunder rang out and rain began to pour down. I tried to cheer Andy up by assuring him I'd find him a pee bottle to use in the tent for the rest of the trip. I stayed up for the next hour wondering where I would find a pee bottle out here in the middle of nowhere.

4
The Big East — An Absolute Slog!

"Remember, a dead fish can float downstream, but it takes a live one to swim upstream."

W. C. FIELDS

An hour into day two's upstream paddle, the Big East River squeezed its banks and the high mounds of sand, topped with mixed woodlands, transformed into the common rocky outcrops capped in giant white pine representative of the Algonquin area. The current quickened, introducing swifts, carpeted with gravel and blocked with medium-size boulders. It was a pinball machine, and Andy and I were the battered steel ball.

This is the portion of the route we'd been warned about. It's where many paddlers attempting the Meanest Link have been injured, given up or both. By mid-morning, I understood why. Upstream travel is challenging. It requires a different mindset — going against the current is unfamiliar to the majority of paddlers. Canoe trips are all about recreation, not using the watershed as a roadway like the voyageurs and Native groups once did. To efficiently travel against the current takes skill.

Andy and I thought we could use a series of lining, eddy-hopping and poling to get ourselves up the Big East. That's what we've done before. Unfortunately, all those textbook maneuvers became meaningless in the Big East's shallow water, and we resorted to merely stepping out of the canoe to wade. Wet feet were the norm as we walked the canoe upriver. Twice we came across other paddlers. Both groups were day-trippers taking advantage of the downstream run from Williamsport Bridge to Arrowhead Provincial Park. Both groups made the same joke. "Hey, you're going the wrong way!"

Very funny.

Andy and I were able to make our way at a snail's pace upriver so long as we stuck close to shore and carefully chose our path in the eddies alongside rapids. Wading and lining can be a very effective way to travel up easy and moderate rapids too strong to paddle up. We just had to read the water correctly.

The going wasn't easy, but the scenery made up for it with mini cascades running down hillsides and valleys crowned in lush green, old growth forest of mixed conifer and deciduous.

The river is not just scenic here, it's teeming with history. First Nation groups navigated it far before European encroachment, loggers flushed squared timber down it, and surveyors marked land for homesteaders. In fact, it was busier with people 100 years ago than it is today.

We visited the Dyer's Memorial monument after pushing up a section of swift water called Bend Rapids. The column of stone was built by Clifton Brown, a lawyer from the United States, and marks the final resting place of his beloved wife, Betsy. The couple honeymooned in Muskoka in 1916 and returned to live here 20 years later, staying along the river in a small cabin. Betsy died in 1956, and her husband had the memorial built with his wife's ashes placed in a stone wall near the peak so she could look over the peaceful river. He spent three years beautifying the area with ponds, walking trails and bridges. Soon after the park area was formed, Clifton died. His ashes were encased in the monument beside Betsy.

As we traveled further east, small rock cliffs dominated the riverbank, squeezing the river and quickening the current. Andy and I lined the canoe up the rapids called Boulder Bash and Sink Hole. We carried across short but unmaintained portages around McArthur Rapids and Lucifer's Ledge. A quarter of the way along the McArthur portage I came upon a discarded stainless-steel water jug. Some poor canoeist must have tied it loosely to their pack and lost it. I'm not sure what the canoeist used to drink from for the rest of the trip, but now Andy had the perfect pee bottle.

We ended our second day at the base of the falls flushing over Distress Dam. It added up to a distance of only 10 kilometers (six miles) for the day, but we couldn't go any further. Our camp was set up in the thick brush at the base of the falls, and we cooked our supper out on the rock ledge above the split cascade. Mosquitoes forced us into the tent as dusk approached. I'd brought a bug shelter on the trip, but we were both too exhausted to bother setting it up.

At dusk, my vertigo kicked in.

A couple of years ago, I was diagnosed with benign positional vertigo. Its effect is a sudden spinning sensation similar to walking off the Tilt-a-Whirl after drinking a bottle of Jack Daniel's. Unpleasant, to say the least. An inner-ear disorder causes it.

Specialists administered drugs, then sent me to physiotherapy, where trained professionals performed a fancy maneuver that involved shaking my head back and forth like a dog with water in its ear.

Doctors said the illness lasts forever and that my hearing will gradually get worse, my balance will depreciate and wilderness canoeing, especially for extended periods, would have to stop.

Being diagnosed with an odd affliction was a shock. The prospect of slowly losing my hearing was upsetting and walking around as if I were drunk most of the time posed some serious challenges. But ending my canoe-tripping career was unacceptable. So, I did what any wilderness-loving paddler would do — I stocked up on the prescriptions I needed and taught myself how to do the head-shaking maneuver while out in the woods.

I rarely get vertigo while on trip. Maybe the illness is stress-related. Maybe wilderness travel is the cure for all. If not, it must be a damn good placebo.

I've seen wilderness trips work health wonders many times. I lead groups of at-risk students on wilderness trips, and I know time spent in the woods is a drug like no other. Take 17-year-old Jason, for example.

On day three of a five-day trip, I found Jason halfway along the portage trail, sitting on his pack, whimpering. The other students in his program passed by without saying much. Each one was battling their own demons on the tough trail, and it didn't help that Jason had made little attempt at forming friendships in the group. He was a loner prone to angry outbursts, and he'd spent the last year self-medicating with pharmaceuticals. Now, at the side of the trail, he was breaking down, and there was little I could do to help him.

The blackflies and lengthy portages weren't Jason's biggest enemy. It was his drug addiction that plagued him.

I'm a wilderness guide and outdoor skills instructor — not a counselor. I feel compassion for each and every one of the students I lead, but my main focus is to teach them the skills needed to keep them safe. I'm not trained to help anyone with personal issues. That said, I've been doing the job so long I've gotten to know a thing or two. Keep your fancy leather couches and high-priced psychobabble; I've witnessed time spent in the wilderness to be an astonishing healer.

Jason just needed more time.

On that third day, Jason was as resentful and as lost as he'd been when we met. He desperately wanted to go home. I had also made a major error in planning the route. I chose a linear trip, not a loop. As we began to make our way back, the students recognized the landscape we were traveling through. Suddenly the trip didn't feel so remote.

It was midnight when Jason escaped. He slipped a canoe into the water and quietly paddled off into the darkness. Luckily, one of the students was sneaking a smoke by the smoldering campfire and came to warn me that Jason was making a run for it.

I went after him. What Jason lacked in paddling skill he made up for in desperation, channeling his anger and loneliness into fast and forceful strokes. I couldn't catch him. He paddled and portaged across two lakes before the storm hit. The pounding rain and strong wind drove him to shore.

When I caught up to him, he was hunkered under a tree, desolate. I put a tarp up, lit a fire and just sat beside him, not saying a word. It was now 2 a.m. We passed the night together, sitting just like that.

At first light, we got back in our boats and paddled to meet our group. Jason admitted he'd taken ecstasy, a street drug usually associated with wild parties and frenetic dancing, and that he'd been high when he paddled away from camp.

No wonder I'd had trouble keeping pace with him. I didn't question, chastise or judge him, but I did suddenly find myself laughing. The juxtaposition. Here we were paddling on a crystal-clear lake, white-throated sparrows welcoming the day and the brightening sky streaked with mare's tail. This was my ecstasy.

Reunited with our group, we spent our remaining two days traveling towards home. Jason didn't try to escape again. It might have been my imagination, but I think I even glimpsed a solitary smile. Not long after the trip, my colleague told me he'd heard through the grapevine Jason had enrolled into a post-secondary outdoor education program. Cool, I thought. It's been a few years since, and recently Jason sent me an email. Now he's got a job taking at-risk students into the woods.

Undoubtedly, there are many people for whom medication and therapy are the best options — but give someone a paddle, canoe and some real time in the wilderness, and I'll show you some natural healing.

5
The End Is Near

*"Out of suffering have emerged the strongest souls;
the most massive characters are seared with scars."*

KAHLIL GIBRAN

We packed up camp early on day three. We needed to get away from the dense fog of bugs. Mosquitoes are expected in June, but I'd never seen them this bad.

We had a quick breakfast of coffee and granola and started to portage around the Distress Dam before 8 a.m., making our way across Distress Lake in the early morning mist. It was a nice break to paddle without fighting a current. But it was short-lived. Distress Lake is just a pocket of calm sludge water, clogged with submerged tree stumps. Once we reached the other side we continued wading up swifts and lifting over ledges.

Our map showed a 1,200-meter (1,312-yard) portage to avoid McBrien Rapids. Finding the starting point wasn't easy, however. Andy and I ended up pulling the canoe and gear up a sandbank when we couldn't walk against the current anymore. From there we continued uphill, pushing through dense balsam trees until we reached a dirt road. Even the road ended a few hundred meters later, with an iron gate and a giant No Trespassing sign. A brushed over side trail got us back to the river and we waded up more rapids to get us to McBrien Pond.

It was a glorious spot. We were entering what's geologists call the Algonquin Dome — the part of Ontario between Georgian Bay and the Ottawa Valley. The landscape reminded Andy and me of northern

Ontario's Algoma region, neighboring the eastern shore of Lake Superior. Distant hills, forested valleys, clear water, and no one to bother us — except, perhaps, the jealous boyfriend of a half-nude sunbather.

Prior to departure, Algonquin Outfitters' Gord Baker had piqued our interest with tales of a local bathing beauty who loved to bask in the sun along the banks of the Big East River without a stitch of clothes on. We weren't sure if Gord was having some fun with us — was it a true tale of erotica or an urban legend to help lonely paddlers get through the nasty parts of the river? The chances of seeing a naked woman in the middle of nowhere were slim, Andy and I reasoned. But that didn't stop us from peering around every bend hoping to spot the boobies of the Siren of the Big East, as we called her.

Three days later it happened. We rounded a river bend and there she was. Our jaws dropped, like pre-teen boys catching a glimpse of an angelic nude during a school field trip to the art museum. So enamored, we didn't notice her male friend sitting on a lawn chair in the shaded woods. Our boyish titters were cut short when we heard a masculine voice bellow out, "Can I help you, boys?" We stared straight ahead and paddled out of there without saying another word.

After crossing McBrien Pond, water levels dropped further and swifts bottomed out into rock gardens. At times we even strapped the packs to our backs while wading to give the canoe more freeboard. There were mixed moments of drudgery and pleasure. Most of this section couldn't be paddled. We just kept walking the canoe up current. Sometimes it was ankle deep, other times I plunged up to my waist. It didn't matter. We just chose to walk rather than paddle.

Finlayson Pond is the last bit of flat water to paddle on the Big East. It's more of a widening in the river than a pond. A dam once operated here back in the 1880s, built by the lumbermen to help with the annual log drives down the river. Distress Dam and McBrien Dam were also constructed at that time. In 2001, the Finlayson Dam was removed. Since then, water levels and the surrounding landscape have been allowed to go back to their natural state. This little bit of history may seem mundane to some, but to me, it's a perfect example of how time can heal all wounds.

The Big East River drops 88 meters (96 yards) along its 50 kilometers

(31 miles), from Algonquin Park to Lake Vernon. Most of the elevation drop is along the upper section. It's also where a number of tributaries enter; cold-water streams such as Tasso, Cripple, Beanpod, Mink and McCraney. The creeks flush down from the surrounding hills and narrow valleys and into Finlayson Pond. What this meant for us, of course, is the going got even tougher after Finlayson Pond. Wading up the stronger current was brutal. The distance on the map measured less than two kilometers to reach our turnoff point at McCraney Creek. But it took an entire afternoon to drag the canoe upriver that whole distance. The closer we got to McCraney, the rockier and shallower the rapids became.

We slowed to a turtle's pace to make sure neither of us got injured. This would not be an ideal spot to call for help. I doubt a rescue team could even have reached us. The saving grace, however, is that past loggers couldn't reach this area either. The steep terrain made it impossible for horse teams to haul logs down to the river. Even today's loggers haven't bothered. Stands of massive white spruce, eastern hemlock, sugar maple, white and yellow birch and some of the most massive white cedar trees I've ever seen remain on the riverbank. The average age of the trees here is 150 to 180 years old.

The mouth of McCraney Creek marks the way out of the Big East River basin and the way to cross over into Algonquin Provincial Park. It's also the most cursed section of the Meanest Link route. Many "Linkers" abandon the route here. The problem is how to get to McCraney Lake.

There are three options, and none are pleasant. The most recent addition is the best choice. In 2014, two portages were cleared and marked by legendary park employee Greg MacDonald. He worked for Ontario Parks for 47 years and had a passion for rediscovering ancient canoe routes. The first portage was marked from the Big East, just downstream of McCraney Creek, to Hood Lake, measuring 1,089 meters (1,191 yards). The second portage was from Hood to McCraney Lake, measuring 1,371 meters (1,499 yards).

These portages weren't cleared when Andy and I did our trip. So we only had two options. The traditional way involved wading up McCraney Creek to the dam at the south end of McCraney Lake. The second option was a bush portage up and over something called Buzzkill Mountain.

AN EPIC CANOE JOURNEY

The first attempt of the Meanest Link was in 2004. Algonquin Outfitters staff members Will Lougheed and Randy Pielsticker set out in early November but cut their trip short upon reaching McCraney. The weather was terrible, the water too low and their food was running out. The next attempt was in June of 2005 by four women — Janet Thomas, Jaime Capell, Sarah Strickland and Leah Sanders. They were the first to complete the entire Link as a continuous canoe trip and finished it in 15 days. They noted McCraney Creek was their absolute low point, and where they almost gave up.

Subsequent Meanest Link groups followed the women's route, including boys from Camp Pathfinder, and they too came back with horror stories of McCraney Creek. It seems the tough part about using the creek to reach McCraney Lake are the water levels, they are even lower than the Big East River. The stream bed is rockier, and the shoreline is steeper. Logs are strewn across the tributary like a giant game of pick-up-sticks.

The second option, over Buzzkill Mountain, was explored just a couple years before our trip by a gang of six Linkers. They chose to push just a little further up the Big East, past where McCraney Creek comes in from the left and Mink Creek comes in from the right. From there, they located an old logging road crossing the river, used it to portage into Hood Lake, and then proceeded to bush crash two kilometers (1.2 miles) up and over the steep rise to McCraney Lake. They were successful, and from the account, it seemed slightly easier than gnarly McCraney Creek.

Andy and I decided to try the second option. Finding the road wasn't easy for us, though. The water was too low past McCraney Creek to wade. We had to portage the packs and canoe along the slimy wet rocks of the riverbed. To make matters worse, it began to rain, making the footing even more slippery. It's a pure miracle neither of us broke any limbs clambering over the last set of rapids. This was a low point for me. My portage pack was wet from all the water sloshing back and forth in the bottom of the boat, adding on a good deal of weight, and I found it impossible to lift the load without Andy's help.

We reminded each other we were turtles on this trip, not rabbits. Many trippers attempting this route act like rabbits, trying to complete the circle around the park as fast as possible. Many are powered by youthful exuberance or male bravado.

The turtle philosophy got us to the road safe and sound an hour later. We guessed where it might be and then hauled the canoe and gear up the riverbank, through dense brush and over a cluster of downed trees. Camp three was pitched right on the old abandoned road. Andy and I took a couple of ibuprofen painkillers each and made a quick dinner before bed. We crawled into the tent before the bugs began to swarm for their nightly feeding frenzy, and Andy made sure he brought in his pee bottle for the night. I grabbed the whisky flask and brought it into the tent as well. We both figured a double shot of rations was in order and made a cheers to what we were now calling the Meanest Hoax.

6
Entering Algonquin — Finally!

*"But a mermaid has no tears,
and therefore she suffers so much more."*

HANS CHRISTIAN ANDERSEN

The morning of day four was spent getting to McCraney Lake and entering Algonquin Park. We kept following the old road, crossed McCraney Creek and eventually veered off to the right and bushwacked our way to Hood Lake. Our time paddling across Hood Lake was slow. Neither of us looked forward to the next portage. With luck, we found flagging tape left by the gang of six Meanest Link paddlers that first found their way over to McCraney Lake via this route. There was no trail at all. We just bushwhacked and glanced at our GPS now and then. A few hundred meters into the dense bush of birch and maple saplings, and the elevation steepened. It was a tough slog from there. To make matters worse, the weather turned humid and deer flies joined the swarms of mosquitoes buzzing around us.

Deer flies, and their bigger cousin, the horsefly, emerge around the same time as black flies are dying off in pre-summer heat and humidity. Changing weather patterns chase off one species of biting insect and invite another. Deer flies are nasty biters, literally taking a chunk of skin to get at your blood. They're also incredibly fast fliers, with a top speed of 108 kilometers (67 miles) per hour. They're impossible to run away from. However, the biggest issue with deer and horse flies is that their bite leaves an open wound that can cause a secondary infection.

Deer flies usually hunt in groups of four or five and are the most common of the two pests. This is a good thing, since horseflies are almost three times the size. The deer fly is slightly larger than a house fly, has a yellow to light brown abdomen with darker stripes, a darker pattern to the wings, and bright green or gold eyes.

They're well known for patiently buzzing around your head until they find a safe place to land, and are mostly attracted to shiny objects, which is why the shimmer of a swimmer's wet back draws them in. This can be their downfall as well. One of the best ways I've learned to fight back is to place a folded piece of Duct tape (sticky side exposed) on the top of my hat. They're attracted to the shine of the tape and the adhesive surface becomes a tomb.

It took another two hours to clamber down to the shores of McCraney Lake. The wailing of a loon welcomed us. We were officially in Algonquin now. The portages would be marked with bright yellow signs, campsites marked with orange triangles, and we'd have thunderboxes, also nicknamed treasure chests, to poop in.

Halfway across McCraney Lake, Andy and I came upon our first park paddlers in the form of a mid-aged couple equipped with a lightweight canoe, matching packs, designer bent-shaft paddles and bright yellow wide-brimmed hats. A white poodle wearing its own designer PFD captained the craft from amidships. Looking at our bedraggled forms with sweat-stained shirts and torn trousers, the man asked how we had accessed the lake from its southern end.

"We just walked up the Big East River; you should try it," Andy said. They didn't respond and let us drift on by.

The central island campsite on McCraney looked inviting. It came complete with a cozy tent pad, a sculpted fire ring, and a makeshift plywood table nailed to two big pine trees. It looked so civilized. Unfortunately, it wasn't even noon, so we continued on and portaged into Rain Lake, following an old road most of the way.

A labyrinth of new and old logging roads lace throughout Algonquin, like tangled fishing line on the bottom of a canoe. Most are hidden from view and closed to the public, but the total distance does add up. According to Wildlands League, there's more than 5,400 kilometers (3,355 miles) of logging roads, adding up to four times the total distance of canoe trails. The city of Toronto doesn't even have that much road. And yes, it's controversial. Algonquin is the only provincial park still actively logged. Proper forest management provides a lot of local employment, but it does detract from the idea of the park being a vast, untapped wilderness.

At the turn of the 20th century, Rain Lake was a bustling place and a main entrance to Algonquin Park. Access was by train via what was then called the Canadian Atlantic Railway. Later, it was renamed the Grand Trunk Railway, and then the Canadian National Railway in 1922.

One of the first cottages in the area was built on Rain Lake by Charles Waterhouse, owner of Huntsville's Deerhurst Lodge. He built it in 1925 as an outpost for fishermen. As more camps were established, Rain Lake's Eagle Lake Landing Railway Station became a put-in for canoeists, located on the southwest shore. A ranger cabin was added in the 1920s. When the railway was abandoned in 1959, an access road was established from the nearby town of Kearney, and another ranger station built at the east end of the lake. The railway bed has since been converted into a section of the park's Western Uplands Hiking Trail.

That night, Andy and I camped on the west side of Rain Lake. Our site came with a slight breeze, so we got naked and went for a dip to wash off the sweat and dirt from hauling up the Big East. It was a nasty time in our lives that we were already beginning to forget.

As we sat naked on a rock slab along the shoreline air-drying ourselves, a canoe approached. We hurriedly got dressed as Randy and Lynn, a local couple who volunteered to bring us our first food drop, approached us. They have brought in supplies for other paddlers on the Meanest Link as well.

"You look better than we expected," Lynn called out as they beached their canoe.

Our visitors were a godsend. Not only did they have a fresh supply of dried food for the next six days — and a new flask of whisky — they also gifted us thick-sliced bacon and massive steaks. We hugged them, even though they were complete strangers. Then hugged them again.

7
Hiding a Paddle

*"Be like a duck. Calm on the surface,
but always paddling like the dickens underneath."*
MICHAEL CAINE

Alone again, fresh bacon replaced our usual breakfast porridge. The hot grease splattered everywhere as it sizzled in the frying pan. Andy shouldered the cooking and I packed up the tent.

Before 9 a.m., Andy and I had portaged out of Rain Lake, heading north. On my way across the portage to Casey Lake, I hid one of two paddles off the trail for Paddle In The Park. It's an annual contest that a group of volunteer canoeists and the owners of Badger Paddles had organized for a good half-dozen years up until 2017. It was created as an incentive to get more people paddling in Ontario parks, as whoever finds the paddle gets to keep it and win a bunch of extra prizes to boot.

I hid the first paddle deep in the muck of a spruce bog and behind a wall of stunted conifer trees. I thought it was hidden well. Once we returned home, I was surprised to learn it had been found the very next day. A second paddle I hid further along on the trip was also found quickly. What surprised me even more was that the majority of paddles hidden that summer by other paddling celebrities had been found by paddlers going on insane, marathon-style day trips. These weekend warriors drove several hours from their urban homes, raced across lakes and portages, frantically searched possible locations in the woods based on clues we provided, then drove back home before sundown.

To me, it had become a type of geocache — not exactly achieving what the contest set out to do, which was to get more people doing overnight canoe trips.

Chris Hocking, a paddler living just north of Algonquin, became what I jokingly referred to as my arch-nemesis. This canoeist found my hidden Paddle In The Park contest paddles three years in a row, yet never once slept in the woods.

Chris found the first paddle I hid during Paddle In The Park's inaugural year in 2013. I stashed it behind a birch tree halfway along the 5,470-meter (5,982-yard) portage heading out of Algonquin's Dickson Lake. Chris drove the 400 kilometers (248 miles) from his home, paddled 16 kilometers (10 miles) of massive Opeongo Lake, portaged three-quarters of the portage trail, found the paddle, then returned home the very same day — all in time for dinner.

The next year, Chris completed a similar feat of endurance. He drove a couple hours from his home, paddled and portaged over 20 kilometers (12 miles) to the very north end of Killarney Provincial Park, and found my paddle hidden along the four-kilometer (2.5-mile) portage leading into Great Mountain Lake. He made it back home in time for dinner once again.

I hid my third paddle between two small ponds in the southern end of Kawartha Highlands Provincial Park. Chris happened to find this one too, and he still hadn't pitched his tent the entire time. Unbelievable!

I later interviewed him for one of my Whisky Fireside Chats for my YouTube channel and gifted him a free tent and sleeping bag, hoping he would take the hint.

Does it matter whether Chris paddles out for a day or spends the night? I think so. Canoe trips have transformative power. However, the key to tapping into this power is to spend time in the wilderness. A weekend jaunt may get you through a bad week at work. A week of paddling may help anxiety levels during moments of crisis. But a two-week canoe trip can offer a Zen moment that lasts for the rest of your life.

As a society, our priorities have changed. In the 1950s, the average canoe trip in Algonquin was a month long. In the 1970s, it was seven to 10 days. In the 1990s, it averaged a week. Now, the standard amount of time spent paddling the interior of the park is two nights. I know life has become insanely busy for most of us, and it's not easy to get away for longer than a mere weekend, but how connected can someone be to their natural surroundings if they're just popping in for a night or two?

I'm a worrier. I worry about people not spending enough time out in the woods. I worry about people being disconnected. I worry no one will have the desire to protect our natural wilderness. With urban sprawl, deforestation and climate change, I worry the next generation won't even have any wilderness left to connect with.

Not only do paddlers trip for shorter periods, more and more canoeing and camping takes place in semi-wilderness parks, which are areas closer to urban centers. Those campers will never know the genuinely magical experiences they're missing — the dark skies, bountiful wildlife and real silence of more remote locations.

Without the opportunity to ever connect to the truly wild areas, who will grow up to love these spaces and fight for them?

8
Those Were the Days

"Take care of all your memories. For you cannot relive them."
BOB DYLAN

After the Rain Lake portage, the plan for the rest of the day was to make our way through a series of small ponds and lesser maintained portages, hugging the western side of the park. The going was easy at first. Places like Hambone, Daisy and Ralph Bice lakes are well-traveled. It was also a time of reminiscing for me. My high school friends and I took countless spring fishing trips through here, keeping to the Petawawa River on our way to lakes like Misty, White Trout, Big Trout, McIntosh and Timberwolf.

Those past trips meant a lot to me. I had more built-up anticipation before each trip than a two-year-old waiting for Christmas morning. The moment the ice broke up on the lakes, we were out paddling to our favorite trout holes. Some years the season came early and we basked in the sun but swatted the blackflies. Other years we dealt with frigid temperatures and freak snowstorms. We relished it all.

Eventually, like with all childhood friendships, life got in the way. We went to college or university, got jobs, married, and had kids. Differences of opinion started to form, and arguments occasionally erupted on trip. We all grew apart, and the Algonquin trips became a cherished memory from the past. Some of us still meet for the odd golf game, and a few got together for a beer at our high school reunion, but I doubt a full week of fishing for trout will ever happen again.

Andy also had memories of past canoe trips here. First with his dad and brother, then his wife. Telling each other stories and reminiscing got us through some of the longer portages, and we pointed out the old campsites and scenic bluffs we remembered. Even though we had changed, the landscape seemed to stay the same. I liked that.

It seems everything was different back then. Those were the days of sleeping on thin blue foam pads, tripping in plaid cotton shirts and wearing denim jeans. Canoes were made of aluminum or fiberglass, and packs had external frames. Dehydrated eggs turned green when cooked and most of the cooking was done over the campfire, not lightweight gas stoves.

Attitudes also were different. We didn't go out on trip to survive or crush a vast distance; we went to relax and thrive. More often, it seems the people who do spend long periods in the wilderness are trying to conquer nature, rather than be part of it. Television's so-called reality shows far outnumber true tales of the joys of wilderness travel. In 2013, Bear Grylls' sensationalistic *Man vs. Wild* was even trumped by the lunacy that is *Naked and Afraid*, which reached nearly four million weekly viewers in its prime.

Quite a few summers ago my daughter Kyla and I went paddling for two weeks across Algonquin. She was seven years old at the time. On the last portage of the trip we met up with a couple of young guys, shouldering monster-size packs and cursing every step of the way. Dressed in full camouflage fatigues, army boots, fake Tilley hats and wearing giant belt knives reaching past their knees, it was apparent this canoe trip was a survival mission. They shared stories of misadventure — it rained, it was windy, bugs had bitten them — and they were deciding whether they should cut their trip short.

"How long you out for?" Kyla asked them.

"This is day one of three full days," one replied, proudly puffing out his chest. When they discovered this was our eleventh day out, their jaws dropped. The young men couldn't comprehend this tiny girl dressed in sneakers, Bermuda shorts and a tattered old t-shirt reading, "I paddle, therefore I am," could take on such a strenuous canoe trip.

"That's a long time for a young girl to be out in the wilderness," one of the overly butch men said. Kyla's response was a thing of beauty, an almost Gandhi-like statement veteran wilderness paddlers would truly appreciate. "You guys obviously don't get out much, do ya?" she asked.

I've never been so proud of my daughter. This is one child not suffering from nature deficit disorder. Kyla's first canoe trip was at the age of six weeks. Our average canoe trip together lasts two weeks, and Kyla wouldn't have it any other way.

Kyla was introduced to canoe tripping at an early age because that's what I do for a good portion of my job. I wouldn't see her much if she didn't go with me. But it wasn't me forcing her out that made her love it so much. Thinking back, my father was a professional boxer, and I hung around a lot of boxing gyms in my youth. That didn't turn me into a lightweight bruiser. Far from it. It was nature itself keeping Kyla's interest. She'll spend countless hours catching and releasing frogs, collecting rocks, talking to loons, and investigating butterflies. She's entirely at peace out there.

A lot has changed over the years of tripping together. Now Kyla carries her own pack, paddles even when no one tells her, sleeps with only one stuffy, and does at least half her camp chores and whittles her own marshmallow sticks.

There are some downfalls, of course. She leaves her bras hanging from the clothesline, gets dramatic over the slightest things, continues to tell me "You wouldn't understand," shaves her legs in my cooking pots and wants to sleep in every morning.

I'll take a few negatives. Kyla is great company. We trip more days together each summer than her friends spend at the beach — and she's proud of it.

I know I'm a lucky dad.

Enjoying wilderness canoe trips together means juggling the roles of protective father, knowledgeable wilderness guide and goofy camp counselor. We sing songs, play games, and bake birthday cakes for no reason. We get down on our hands and knees to look at tiny seedlings and insects on the forest floor, sometimes referencing our field guide if we don't recognize them. And I try to swallow my parental instincts and let her make her own mistakes.

I do all this because Kyla has grown up loving the wilderness and canoe tripping, and I want to keep it that way. The joys and miseries of backbreaking portages and long paddling days can wait until she's older. I want canoe tripping to be fun, so she keeps wanting more. And, so far, it's working.

Most importantly, Kyla is part of each trip we go on, from planning to completion. She's not just tagging along. She's invested in the adventure. I think it's this small bit of ownership in her world, which is dictated by adult-enforced rules, keeping her so in love with it.

There's a stand-up act by comedian Jim Gaffigan on the stupidity of camping. I checked it out on YouTube one night when Kyla was about eight years old. I found the skit amusing, a tongue-in-cheek roast of mummy bags, outhouses and dangerous bears. Kyla did not enjoy it. She gave a severe frown when the comedian opined, "Do you know why my parents never took me camping? Because they loved me!"

Then she demanded I turn the video off. "I feel so sorry for that man," she told me.

She's grown to love the woods even more than I do. And that love has inspired a passionate desire to protect her playground. On a canoe trip in Algonquin at the age of nine, she memorized a quote by Chief Seattle, the 19th-century advocate for wilderness protection and Native rights. One evening, she recited his words to me:

"We are part of the earth, and it is part of us. The flowers are our sisters, the deer, the horse, the great eagle, these are our brothers. The rocky crests, the juices of the meadow, the body heat of the pony and the man, we all belong to the same family. The shiny waters that move through the streams and rivers, is not just water, but the blood of our ancestors."

Someday the blood in the shining water flowing through the streams and rivers will be mine. I have to believe that my grandchildren and the next generation will paddle these waters and will fight to protect them.

9
Always Say Hello

"It's the faces within the trees that always smile and say hello."
ANTHONY T. HICKS

A few hours of paddling and portaging from our Rain Lake campsite found us close to a popular western access point for the park. It's a busy place for weekend warrior types, some less ethical than others. We were reminded of this during the portage from Hambone to Ralph Bice Lake. The well-trodden path had been trashed by a group at the put-in, leaving behind a dozen full Coke cans, bottles of iced tea, jars of jam, a vast assortment of canned food, and a lawn chair. Who would do such a thing?

Not only is it illegal to have cans and bottles in the park — they're crazy heavy to carry. No doubt, this is why the group left everything behind. Worse, this type of garbage attracts bears. I was informed by park staff after our trip a bear did indeed find the food, and then stayed around trying to get more from neighboring campsites. It became such a problem the bear was shot and killed.

Increasingly, it seems there's a self-interested attitude permeating the woods. I see fewer campers leaving behind a bit of firewood for the next person, more trashed campsites and graffiti decorating rock cliffs, and a lot of paddlers who don't even bother to say hello while passing each other on the portage.

Not saying hello is something I don't understand. The problem with ignoring others while traveling in remote wilderness areas, besides being characterized as brash and unmannerly, is that you never know who you might need to call upon for help. It was my father who taught me this. He always insisted I say hello and even have a quick conversation with the people we met in the woods.

My dad's lesson echoed in my head as things turned dire for an ill-fated group of three paddlers I encountered once in late October. Earlier that day, the trio drifted by my canoeing partner and me as we sat in our boat, eating our lunch. They didn't return my friendly gestures. I waved, repeated my jovial "Hello," and asked how their trip was going. They completely ignored me and continued across the lake, not once looking back in my direction.

I wrote them off as snobs who felt that shunning other paddlers in the backcountry is the next best thing to seeing no paddlers at all.

My canoe buddy suggested we snub the nasty trio right back and continue on our way. And we did until we caught up to them, frantically searching for the portage at the end of the lake.

We had unkind inclinations to misguide them towards a false trail, but my conscience took over. I yelled out directions to the correct path. Barely acknowledging us, one paddler motioned back with a half-hearted wave. Another responded bitterly that they already knew the location of the portage. The third continued to disregard our very existence as if we were intruding on their experience. Had they been friendlier, they would have realized I was trying to advise them which fork to take midway down the trail.

We left them to argue, portaged across the unmarked trail and set up camp on the next lake. As we settled in, we were astounded to see the three paddlers crash through the bush and onto the shore — not from the portage access, but from an entirely different direction. They didn't heed our fork-in-the-trail advice. My dad would've said justice had been served. Good riddance!

White-capped waves were forming and the air temperature hovered just above freezing. Back on the water and midway across the lake, the paddlers capsized and yelled for help. Their canoe was overloaded with lawn chairs and a beer cooler, and their clothes and sleeping bags weren't packed in waterproof bags. None wore lifejackets.

AN EPIC CANOE JOURNEY

My canoe mate and I did the right thing. We hopped into our canoe and rescued the group, bringing them to shore to share our campfire and dry off. They were a tad sheepish around camp, but they finally shared a proper hello.

The whole experience got me thinking of an article I wrote for a magazine a few years back on the hermits of the north. I interviewed three individuals who escaped society to live alone in the wilderness. When I asked what they thought would cause the demise of the human species, they all answered the same: self-interest. It wasn't pollution, nuclear holocaust or a zombie apocalypse. It's people not thinking of anyone except themselves.

Algonquin's park staff have noted how visitors to the park are changing. For starters, numbers have significantly increased. At its inception, the only way to experience the park was to canoe in. In 1895, a total of 38 visitors were recorded. Then the railway, built by lumber baron J.R. Booth in 1896, brought fancy resorts and hundreds of visitors to the southern lakes.

Highway 60 was constructed in 1933, bisecting the park. The highway brought in 12,000 campers in 1936. Group camping became a major fad after World War II, and some lodges were removed and campgrounds built instead. In 1948, Highway 60 was paved, bringing even more visitors. By 1956, 21,462 had arrived by car. A year later, 32,557 car campers were recorded. Interior use by canoe trippers grew as well. Between 1958 and 1965 the number of interior campers per year went from 10,000 to 32,000.

During the early years, there were no marked interior campsites or bright yellow portage signs. Canoe trippers pitched camp where they saw fit. Permits to enter and make use of the park weren't required until 1929.

With road access, park rangers started noticing the skill level of campers had decreased. At one time, canoeing in Algonquin was a considerable expedition, one taken by someone with vast wilderness skills or with an expert guide. Increasingly, the park staff had to tell everyone where to camp, portage, and even where to poop. Latrines were introduced to interior sites in 1931, numbering a few hundred. Now there are 1,900 campsites marked and maintained in the backcountry.

The interior rangers also attempted to solve the increase in cans and bottles piling up behind the sites by sinking them to the bottom of the lake. In 1969, a whopping $70,000 (the equivalent of almost $500,000 in 2018) was spent to clean up the mess built up since the birth of the park. The rangers collected and hauled out more than 350,000 liters of garbage from the interior, minus what had been sunk in the lakes.

Visitation increased dramatically by the 1970s. Between 1971 and 1976, there were 65,000 paddlers wandering around the interior. Inexperienced baby boomers were coming to Algonquin in droves and leaving their mark. An interior map was produced in 1974 to offer route-planning assistance and information on proper camping etiquette. The year 1975 brought a quota system to help disperse the crowds, and new regulations were rolled out regarding how many people could camp at each site. The number nine was chosen due to youth camps traditionally traveling three per canoe.

A can and bottle ban was introduced in 1978, and yellow garbage bags were handed out to campers bearing the group's permit number. Rangers hoped to stop the littering problem and catch those perpetrators who gathered their garbage only to toss the bag alongside a trail or roadway.

To date, it's still very much a cat and mouse game. There are more paddlers traveling in the interior, a small percentage of whom litter, yet fewer rangers searching for violators. But it's not all doom and gloom. There are far more people loving and cherishing the park than there are ignorant fools who leave their trash at the end of a portage.

10
Butt Lake Becomes Ralph Bice Lake — Thank Goodness

"I got a late start as a trapper because my dad wouldn't let me go alone in a canoe until I was four."

RALPH BICE

I t was a quick paddle across Ralph Bice Lake. Mid-day of day five on the trip, and we were closing in on the 100-kilometer (62-mile) mark. The winds were calm and our next series of portages started halfway along the northwest shore.

Ralph Bice Lake has changed names several times. First, it was named Eagle Lake because eagles once nested on the south shore's cliff face. Then it was renamed Butt Lake because it is situated in Butt Township, named after the prominent Irish nationalist, Sir Isaac Butt. In 1998, the Friends of Algonquin suggested renaming it in honor of Ralph Bice, which to me is a far more meaningful name. I never met Ralph Bice. I never met Sir Issac Butt, either. But I did read Ralph's books cover to cover many times, soaking in his wisdom on what he liked to call bush sense.

Bice was a trapper, writer and Mayor of Kearney, Ontario from 1939 to 1946. He was born 1900 and died in 1997. His most popular book was his memoir titled *Along the Trail in Algonquin Park*, published in 1980. He was also a columnist for the local *Almaguin News* for 30 years and received the Order of Canada in 1985. Sitting beside Pierre Elliott

Trudeau during the awards ceremony, he was quoted telling the Prime Minister he was the "luckiest fellow in the room." When Trudeau asked why, Ralph replied, "Because there is only one trapper in this room and you are sitting next to him."

Like many good writers, he was known for his strong opinions and sharp intellect. He believed that artist Tom Thomson, of the Group of Seven fame, likely drowned on Canoe Lake because he was a drunk or killed himself due to depression. He defended the ethics of trapping and believed trappers were the "true caretakers of nature." He also hated when the government changed the names of lakes and, ironically, would have much rather seen Ralph Bice Lake keep its original Eagle Lake name.

Ralph Bice's first canoe trip in Algonquin was at the age of 12 with his park ranger father. They stayed at his grandfather's cabin on Roseberry Lake, the same place his father based himself out of in 1888 to hunt deer. Ralph took his first guiding job at age 17 and spent the night prior alone, curled under a blanket along a marshy creek, hearing wolves gather around him. He told author Bill Steer about his first trip in a memorable interview just before his death. "I just rolled into my blankets and fell asleep, tired and hungry. Several times during the night I heard the wolves howl right at the edge of the timber, and to a 17-year-old boy it seemed like the whole pack was headed my way."

Steer added that to him, it was "a time of exuberant youth that made way towards his lifetime of knowledge, skills and attitudes towards wilderness travel."

Alan Pope, a former Ontario minister of natural resources, once wrote of the infamous Algonquin trapper, "Hunting guide, outdoorsman, trapper, writer, raconteur extraordinaire, Ralph Bice has come to symbolize the pioneering spirit of Algonquin." Some of Northern Ontario's most colorful figures were part of Ralph's life, including lumber king J.R. Booth, painter Tom Thomson, and famous English renegade, Archie Belaney, later to become known as Grey Owl. Ralph Bice was the guide chosen to take the Governor General and the Duke of Devonshire into Algonquin Park in 1918.

11
A Bump in the Night

"Fear can make a moth seem the size of a bull elephant."
STEPHEN RICHARDS

Our next camp was a small site on quaint Iagoo Lake. It hadn't been used for quite a while. Grass grew out of the fire ring, and the tent pad was overgrown with blueberry bushes. We liked camping there, though. It was a peaceful place, away from the business of the larger lakes to the south. We also had our first camp visitor. A small deer mouse tried to enter the tent around midnight. I was half asleep and mistook the noise for something larger and let out a high-pitched scream. Andy teased me to no end.

On each trip, it takes me a few nights to settle in. The first night every sound seems creepy and I worry a bear could terrorize my camp at any moment. By night five I'm too exhausted to worry about bears ripping through my tent.

I once pitched my tent in the old Cobourg Jail, located about an hour-and-a-half drive east of Toronto. It's considered one of the most haunted places in Ontario. Why would I do something so foolish? To fight my fears, of course.

A radio show wanted me to discuss the increasing number of phobias keeping people out of the woods and from ever sleeping in a tent. I hoped my sleepover in the haunted jail would help listeners learn how to deal with their own fears of the unknown. Rather than being spooked by bears or bad weather, I'd be dealing with haunting cries from the spirit world. No problem.

I thought it was a cool idea at first. I'm not a big believer in the paranormal, but my daughter was impressed that I was willing to spend a night with the undead. Then I found out how truly haunted the place is supposed to be. Clairvoyant mediums from around the world have come to the Cobourg Jail to communicate with ghosts. There are countless reports of strange noises, floating orbs and an all-around sense of spookiness. The depths of prison — the dreaded basement, complete with solitary confinement cells — is where most of the bad vibes originate. Though the jail has been renovated into an inn and many guests have stayed in the themed guest rooms, no one is permitted to spend a night alone in the belly of the beast. That's where I'd be sleeping for the entire night. Alone.

People suffering from a camping phobia might have the same symptoms I expected to feel during my night in the haunted jail. Physical and psychological anxiety can cause someone to sweat, become nauseous, raise their blood pressure, feel a tightening in the chest and experience difficulty breathing.

I'm a strong believer in the philosophy of facing your fears to cure what ails you. Fear and anxiety are a part of everyone's life. We are all afraid of something, whether it's bear attacks, ghosts or just eating broccoli. Avoiding the things we're afraid of is also normal, and a form of self-preservation. But while we can all live normal lives without facing our fears of ghosts and broccoli, having a life with no connection to the natural world isn't healthy.

Sleeping in a haunted jail cell and talking about it on the radio would not only help me relate to those nighttime fears many first-time campers have; but I also hoped it might inspire a few people to spend a night facing their own fears in the woods.

Regrettably, I listened to a few local ghost stories before my sleepover in jail. That was a bad idea. The local Peterborough Paranormal Group warned me of demons disguising themselves as children, powerful energy that could move me across the room and spirits possessing both me and my camping gear. They also warned me of the witching hour, a moment during the night when the spirits are more active; usually around 3 a.m.

Everything went well at first. The double shot of Jack Daniel's before bed made me fall asleep fairly quickly. At 3:02 a.m., however, I was woken up by some loud bangs and thumps. I felt a strong energy source pulsing outside my thin nylon tent, just outside the circle of sea salt the paranormal group gave me to create a protective barrier.

"Go away. I'm not afraid of you," I called out.

My reaction is similar when a bear wanders into camp — and it seemed to work. All went quiet for a moment. A few seconds later, I felt the energy pulse beneath me, as if it was trying to lift my body off the damp basement floor. Then there was a soft push from below — that just creeped me right out.

I flicked on my lantern. It flickered and went out. Strange, since I'd put new batteries in it before I went down to the basement. I turned on my backup flashlight, a small LED light from my camera bag. My fear got the best of me. My anxiety level grew. I was nauseous, and my heart pounded. It's probably exactly what happens when a new camper thinks every noise beyond the tent is a marauding bear — and it ends up being a harmless field mouse. This time I bellowed, "Go away. I'm not afraid of you!" The odd surge of energy decreased and faded away.

In retrospect, I think all my fears were playing on my subconscious — waking me up right at the witching hour and making me feel something outside my tent. Of course, nothing came of it.

That's not to say I ever want to sleep in the Cobourg Jail again. That would be just foolish. The place is definitely haunted.

12

Moose Pee on the Campsite

*"Hunters will tell you that a moose is a wily
and ferocious forest creature. Nonsense.
A moose is a cow drawn by a three-year-old."*

BILL BRYSON

We portaged more than we paddled on our sixth day of the trip, carrying over seven kilometers on mostly uphill trails. The more remote upper north-western section of the park is less traveled and made up of mini ponds, babbling brooks, longer portages and roughed-out campsites. Little maintenance had been done to the mud-filled, brushed-over portages. It was still a nice place to be. The lakes (Papukeewis, Mama, Shaw-Shaw, Tim) were small and secluded, and the forest was made up of thick stands of hardwood.

Algonquin is made up of two different forest zones, split by a lofty dome of Precambrian rock. To the east, it's flat with sandy soil and predominately red and white pine trees. The west side features the highlands, a much more elevated and moister environment. Here, the forest is made up of sugar maple, American beech and yellow birch.

Before the loggers arrived, white pine also towered above the clumps of deciduous. Now the forest is primarily second-and-third-growth hardwood, with the odd old-growth pine tree ignored by the lumberman's axe.

Andy and I stopped for lunch on an island in the northeast corner of Tim Lake, named after Algonquin's first chief ranger, Tim O'Leary. Lunch was routine to us by now. We'd pull up to shore and find a flat rock along the water's edge to snag a breeze and calm the bugs. I'd break apart the bannock made the night before while Andy carved up the cheese and dried meat. Lunch was a simple meal. Sometimes we'd treat ourselves and unpack the stove for some tea or hot soup, but it was rare. Usually, we'd refill our water jugs and sprinkle in some juice crystals or throw in a small slice of lemon and a bit of brown sugar. Before packing up and heading on our way again, we'd unfurl the maps and glance over our route for the afternoon.

Life was simple. That's what I love about a canoe trip. You spend the day moving from one point to another, carrying all your belongings with you. After a few days of traveling, you and your canoe partner have told and retold so many stories that most of the day is made up of just hand and face gestures rather than idle chit-chat. We'd pause in unison to catch a glimpse of a moose feeding in a back bay or listen to the wail of a loon. Six days in, and we were as in sync as an old married couple on their 50th wedding anniversary.

To reach the Nipissing, where we'd begin to head east downriver, we paddled and portaged through yet another series of lakes that receive little maintenance (Chibiabos, West Koko, Big Bob). Finally reaching the Nipissing and pointing the bow of the canoe downstream felt euphoric. Well over a hundred kilometers in, we knew the hardest part was behind us.

I've grown to love the Nipissing. I've paddled this river several times, building fond memories of fishing its feisty brook trout and paddling under majestic old-growth pine.

It's not much of a river at first — to be honest, it's more of a sodden field of sedge grass with a shallow channel of water trickling through it. This was Andy's first time seeing the river, and he was not overly impressed. He didn't say much when we viewed it from the portage. He just threw the packs into the canoe, pushed us into the slack current and asked where all the moose were. Before our trip I had enticed him with stories of paddling under giant pine and spotting abundant moose.

We spotted the first one five minutes later, dead and rotting in the river. Here the waterway was twisted, a wall of alder bushes clogging it. It was taking forever to gain any distance and it was late in the day, with the mosquitoes coming out in full force.

It was just before dusk when we finally spotted a designated spot to pitch our tent, a hump of dry land just beyond where the river empties out of Grass Lake. Unfortunately, it was already taken by a giant bull moose. We were desperate to make camp, so Andy and I yelled out a few swear words and banged our paddles on the side of the canoe. Our scare tactics were moderately successful. The moose slowly wandered off, but not before urinating directly on the tent pad area.

It was dark by this point, so we gave up on a campfire and put our sleeping bags in the bug shelter. We pitched it along the riverbank rather than place our tent directly in a pool of moose pee.

The bug shelter I packed was a welcomed piece of gear. It's a regular eight- by 10-foot tarp but with a veil of no-see-um netting hanging down on all sides. With the four corners guyed out to trees and the bottom pegged down, the majority of biting insects can't find their way in. It became our sanctuary most nights. We ate in it, drank our nightly whisky in it, and sometimes even slept in it.

Andy and I had just finished our second dram of spirits and were about to get snug in our sleeping bags when the jumbo bull moose returned. He was slowly making his way upriver, past our campsite, feeding on water plants as he went. It was too dark to actually see him; we just heard the bull plod through the water, stopping now and then to plunge into the depths of the river to feed. Not long after, we heard a second moose, then a third. The Nipissing was alive with hungry moose. By morning a total of seven moose had wandered past our camp, eating horsetail, sedge and pond weeds as they went.

Moose are abundant in the park. Recent counts number them between 3,000 to 4,000, and the Nipissing is one of the regular hangouts for them. What did surprise us was seeing two deer the next morning. Deer are less common in the park, and moose prefer this arrangement. Deer are carriers of a parasitic brain worm harmless to them but deadly to moose. The parasite transmits via slugs or snails lying in the grass, which are consumed by accident when moose feed. Death is a slow process. The moose becomes weak, blind and emaciated. It begins to walk in circles, repeatedly tilts its head back and forth, staggers and becomes fearless — sometimes picking fights with humans, cars and freight trains.

White-tail deer once dominated Algonquin. Traditional logging practices and the suppression of forest fires destroyed the old forest, opening up a buffet of new saplings. Just have a look at all the vintage photos from the early 1950s of tourists feeding deer along Highway 60. However, by the 1970s, the forest aged and the deer became non-existent. Moose photos were the norm by the mid-1980s.

Algonquin had such a surplus of moose that the park even traded some. In 1985, the park gave the Upper Peninsula of Michigan in the United States 29 moose in exchange for 150 wild American turkeys. The moose were drugged, blindfolded, their ears plugged, then given a ride in a giant sling dangling below a helicopter. Once extracted from the park's interior they were weighed, measured, collared, ear-tagged, and given a shot of antibiotics and a pregnancy test before being trucked to Michigan.

I remember watching it all unfold on the news. It was like watching a rerun of *Mutual of Omaha's Wild Kingdom* television show from the 1960s. In all, 10 bulls and 19 cows — all except one were pregnant — were sent off to Michigan. Five didn't survive the transfer. I wonder if the turkeys fared as well.

More Algonquin moose were traded in 1987. The moose did much better than the beavers, the first species the park trapped and shipped out. In 1908, several beavers were live-trapped and sent to zoos and animal collectors all over the world. It was a publicity stunt undertaken in hopes of getting more people to come to Algonquin. Unfortunately, most of the beavers died during transport and park officials abandoned the idea by 1918.

Historically, park management has brought in more wildlife species than it has taken out. During the early years, some staff biologists believed the more animals Algonquin boasted, the more tourists would visit and the more revenue the park would generate. In 1912, 10,000 smallmouth bass were introduced to the Madawaska watershed because many anglers didn't have the patience or skill to catch a trout. They quickly spread to other lakes in the park and immediately started to out-compete natural brook trout for the same food sources. In the same decade, pheasants were released as well as large European grouse, neither of which survived.

In 1935, 10 elk were introduced. Caribou would have been next, but when all the elk died by 1949 and the project was abandoned.

Before a new species was welcomed, some of the competing native species were exterminated to make ecological room for the newcomers. In 1894, a visiting park superintendent of the Niagara Falls Park, James Wilson, suggested that the park wage war against loons — he referred to them as commercially unimportant birds — to protect the trout population. He also advised that "bears and foxes should be destroyed without mercy." But it was the wolves that park officials truly set out to exterminate. The reason was simple enough back then — kill the main predator of the park to protect "every desirable form of animal life."

For a good many years after the park's creation, every new superintendent dreamed of exterminating wolves from the area. Each tried to figure out a new state-of-the-art way to destroy the canids. Strychnine poison was placed in deer carcasses, but only until rangers realized that other animals feeding on the deer died too, including bald eagles, ravens, grey jays, minks and foxes. Snare wire was a popular method. In 1931, rangers reported 128 wolves killed. It was noted snares were also killing deer, the species the park officials were trying to protect by killing wolves. Shooting wolves was difficult. The wolves soon learned the range of the rangers' rifles, and stayed clear.

None of the killing practices were efficient. The wolves were just too darn smart. In 1934, park superintendent Frank McDougall, later appointed Deputy Minister of the Department of Lands and Forests, questioned the policy of ridding Algonquin of its top predator. He noticed many deer frozen and dead alongside the railway. Left unchecked by its main predator, the deer were overpopulated and vulnerable to disease and starvation.

In 1959, the killing of wolves in Algonquin stopped, and the protection of the species has come a long way since. However, it's been a convoluted ride.

In 2001, all hunting of wolves and coyotes was banned in the 40 townships surrounding the park to create a large buffer zone. Wolf populations had been dropping dramatically, even faster than when the park was poisoning, snaring and shooting them. One of the main hypotheses was that wolves were being hunted and trapped just outside the park boundary.

Things became even more complicated when biologists discovered Algonquin's wolves are Eastern Wolves (Canis lycaon) related to the red wolf (Canis rufus), which is protected under the Endangered Species Act in the United States. Previously, it was believed park wolves were gray wolves (Canis lupus), related to those found in northern Canada. Park biologists started questioning whether the wolves should be protected beyond the park and buffer zones as well.

To make the matter more difficult, it's believed the Eastern Wolf may be in decline due to breeding with coyotes, and northern Gray wolves. Hybridization decreases the genetic diversity of the original species. It also makes the species very difficult to protect because they're hard to identify.

In 2016, the Eastern Wolf was renamed the Algonquin Wolf, recognizing its genetic distinctiveness, and it went from a "species of special concern" to designated as "threatened" under the Ontario Species at Risk Act. There are estimated to be just under 500 Algonquin wolves. Protected areas expanded to Killarney Provincial Park, Kawartha Highlands Provincial Park and Queen Elizabeth Wildlands Provincial Park, as well as townships surrounding those parks.

Some biologists say this still might not be enough. Many experts believe Algonquin's wolves need to expand their range far more to enrich their genetic diversity. Staying in the boundaries of the parks and buffer zones may not be the best protective strategy in the long run.

As my old progressive professor at forestry school said back in the early 1980s: "Islands of protection can quickly become islands of extinction." He was smirked at by all his college colleagues back then. They viewed him as one of the most uneducated, disrespected, wolf-loving educators we had lecturing us. It was a different time back then. Back then, some of my classmates believed I was gay simply because I was reading Aldo Leopold's *A Sand County Almanac*. Thinking back, I think that professor was one of the most memorable prophets of my time. And, by the way, the same college now has Leopold's book on the required reading list for first-year students.

Another point that's made by wolf biologists is that even if the extra protection given to wolves in 2016 works, physically safeguarding them in those specific areas is easier said than done. Not only is it difficult to tell an Algonquin Wolf and coyote apart, or to ever figure out if it's a hybridization of the two; there are hunters and trappers who simply don't like the idea of protecting the species in the first place. And even if hunters and trappers agreed with the protection, the only way it would work would be to add the coyote to the protected list as well, so coyotes and wolves never get mixed up at a distance. It's hard to imagine 100 percent approval on that.

Algonquin's Nature Interpreters have been organizing wolf howls for the general public along the Highway 60 corridor since 1963. Each one gets around 2,500 campers lined up along the roadside, waiting for a pack of Algonquin Wolves to answer back. I think the main draw is the primeval sound, which reconnects people to the wilderness. However, in 2014, 2015, 2017 and 2018 all scheduled howls were canceled. No wolves were answering back.

13

Homesick on the Nipissing

"I don't think the homesickness of a perpetual wanderer can ever be quenched."

SASHA MARTIN

The Nipissing squeezed in a little more after Loontail Creek. It also stopped twisting so much. Patches of alder bushes no longer blocked the way, and large white pines shaded the riverbank, rooted on top of sand and granite. The portages were short but not well maintained, and we encountered a few log jams to lift our canoe over. The changing scenery impressed Andy more. Trout snatched up emerging mayflies and we spotted two more moose and a deer by the time we reached High View Cabin.

The cabin is at the end of a portage on the left bank of where the river makes a dramatic turn to the east. It was built here in 1922, amongst the much larger buildings of the J.R. Booth lumber camp. Park rangers used it while on fire patrol. It was burnt down by a lightning strike in 1928 while the rangers were out picking up a new recruit and rebuilt the same year. Most of the material to build the structure was gathered from the neighboring lumber camp, making the cost a mere $37.50 of the $50 budget.

Rangers were hired in Algonquin to protect the wildlife, fight forest fires and to keep an eye on the loggers. Timber was cut in the new park, but the rangers wanted to make sure it was done correctly. The loggers were also notorious for illegally hunting and trapping game.

Life wasn't easy for the first rangers. Trapping wasn't allowed in the newly established park, and the men who had annual trap lines in the region had been running them for 30 to 40 years in some cases weren't happy about the new regulations. One of the first to rebel was Isaac Bice, grandfather of Ralph Bice, the well-known writer and onetime head of the trapper's association. He had a cabin and trapline set up on Roseberry Lake, just south of where Loontail Creek meets the Nipissing River. Some trappers turned to violence while protesting the new rules. Isaac didn't. He simply informed the park he would need to trap his line for one more winter to prevent his family from starving. "Catch me if you can!" he said. They did catch him, and Isaac served three weeks in jail, becoming the first trapper to be convicted of poaching in Algonquin Park.

Another catch-me-if-you-can story is that of Archie Belaney, a trapper who later became the infamous Grey Owl, an Englishmen who disguised himself as a Native and became a world-renowned writer and conservationist. In March of 1908, the chief park ranger gave the go-ahead for rangers to trap beaver to gather revenue for the park while maintaining a ban on poaching. This decision infuriated Belaney. He was an active trapper well before he became a legendary conservationist. Belaney bet the park staff he could cross Algonquin to trap that winter without being caught.

Belaney didn't get far. He left from Dorset on the western side of the Park and was discovered a few days later by rangers on patrol between Smoke and Ragged Lake. As the story goes, Belaney fell through the ice while crossing a small pond south of Tea Lake. In the middle of the night he walked into their camp, a shelter hut constructed along the portage, with badly frozen feet and asked the rangers for help. They did and took him out to the Canoe Lake hut where they continued to mend his feet for several days. Belaney wasn't the famous Grey Owl then, but the rangers remarked that the prisoner kept the men entertained with stories while his frozen feet healed.

Andy and I had booked High View Cabin for the night, but it was only mid-day when we arrived. It was a humid day and hundreds of mosquitoes were buzzing around. We decided to continue downstream, missing out on one of Nipissing's biggest charms, but stopped to peek inside first.

Moose antlers and cross-cut saws furbished the outside walls, while a wood stove and plywood bunks made up the interior decor. Graffiti was everywhere. Some scribbles were from anglers a few decades back when Algonquin's interior cabins didn't require reservations. It was first-come, first-serve. Other inscriptions were recent, some from youth camps and others from park maintenance crews. Amongst them was Andy's son, Sean Baxter. He was part of the interior maintenance crew and we had just missed him by a few days.

Seeing his son's name etched into the cabin bunk made Andy homesick. The two have a strong bond forged during past canoe trips. Andy and his wife have taken their son and two daughters canoe tripping since they were toddlers. To see Sean spending his summer working in the woods put a smile on Andy's face, but also made him feel absent from his son's life. I offered the use of my satellite phone so he could call home. Doing so was officially against our rules of the trip, as the phone was only for emergencies and a few interviews I had planned with CBC Radio. But a few minutes of battery juice wouldn't be an issue. Andy made a quick call, told his wife about Sean's signature, and handed me back the phone.

I was surprised that Andy agreed to use the phone. He's against technology out in the woods, and always has been. He's one of the last paddlers I know who bought themselves a GPS, and he cringes when someone packs an iPad on trip. Something made him switch character that night, however.

I chalked it up to getting close to the halfway point of the trip. That's when trippers start thinking of home, jobs, friends and kids. Homesickness is the norm for many during the halfway point, and Andy was hit hard that night. We even considered ending the trip early, looking at the maps while in camp and planning an escape route. The mosquito population didn't help matters. They were brutal at the campsite we chose for the night.

We set up the bug shelter, ate a cold dinner and had our nightly supply of whisky early. The evening entertainment was watching a snapping turtle slowly make its way from the river up a sandy bank. I poured the whisky, and Andy timed the turtle. It took two drams of blended malt and 23 minutes for the turtle to make it to the top. The moment the slow-moving reptile reached the peak, it leaned the wrong way and went tumbling back down to the river. We giggled at the poor turtle's misfortune and took it as a sign to keep to our planned route, in keeping with the tortoise and hare analogy of course.

Looking back, I'm shocked that Andy and I even considered finishing the trip early. We never end a trip early. It's one of our golden rules. That's why we get along. We're there for the same reasons: the pure joy of being immersed in the wilderness for as long as possible.

I'm generally a happy person, and the happiest when out in the woods. That's why the media dubbed me The Happy Camper years ago. Having such a cheerful stage name is a good thing, except when I'm not happy, of course. It's true; I have a dark side that shows its devilish face now and then.

I don't mind trudging up long, rocky and buggy portages. I'm not unhappy eating porridge for the fifth morning in a row. I don't even mind being chased off lakes by lightning. These are unavoidable circumstances. These and the other elements of outdoor adventure are the challenges I enjoy overcoming. Without these adversities, I would not have as many fond memories.

What does make me an unhappy camper is when a campmate does something immoral. I'm sure I'm not alone here. Call these behavioral faux pas pet peeves, personal vexations, disgruntlements or whatever. But here, in rough order of magnitude, are a few ways to piss off The Happy Camper.

Let's begin with the mild irritants. Having a paddling partner arrive late at the access point — doing so without good reason or apology bumps this up a level. Not paying an equal share of trip costs. Not doing one's fair share of camp chores. And at the top of this list, continually complaining about the unalterable weather.

Then there are the moderately annoying tendencies which include, in no particular order: yelling "There's a moose" and watching it run away before anyone can get a camera out; carrying less than me but complaining about the weight; constantly comparing gear choices and extolling the virtues of theirs over mine.

I'm also not a big fan of people sneaking into my supply of gummy worms and eating the Smarties from my stash. I don't like it when someone borrows my toothbrush and doesn't tell me about it until the last day. Or when you run out of toilet paper, then use my supply in outrageously generous amounts. Or when you critique how I run rapids, start fires, hang the food or make and clean up meals.

Pooping too close to camp is just wrong. Not digging a deep enough hole is gross and lazy. Singing the same song over and over again is okay if you're Johnny Van Zant of Lynyrd Skynyrd. Otherwise, it's annoying. Why would you use a sharp metal knife to cut the cake I baked in my non-stick coated pan? And then there is getting hurt while showing off and whining about it while I have to take care of you.

The absolute worst — worse than littering and blocking the put-in of a portage, worse than dog owners who don't control their dogs, and even more bothersome than having the camp cook not wash his hands — is being obsessed about completing the planned route sooner than expected.

I am a really, really unhappy camper when I'm with a person who is determined to rush through a canoe trip, which took us weeks to plan and involved much pondering about route choices and gear options. After days, weeks and months spent waiting to escape from the crazed normality of day-to-day life, it makes no sense to race through the wilderness and finish a trip early. A seven-day canoe trip is a seven-day canoe trip. Why turn a seven-day trip into a five-day trip? So you can go back to the rat race you were trying to escape in the first place?

I'll be sleep-deprived and grumpy if you snore. I'll be irritable if you drink all my whisky. But I'll be the extremely unhappy camper if you shorten our time in the woods.

14
The Trojan Horse

*"I'll tell you a secret. Something they don't teach you in your temple.
The Gods envy us. They envy us because we're mortal, because
any moment might be our last. Everything is more beautiful
because we're doomed. You will never be lovelier than you are now.
We will never be here again."*

DAVID BENIOFF (Achilles in the movie *Troy*, 2004)

The mosquito population seemed to have tripled in numbers at camp that night. I've never experienced mosquitoes so bad. We later discovered it was a record year for biting bugs due to the very wet spring creating perfect hatching conditions. It was a good thing that Andy had perfected his nightly pee bottle routine. I had resorted to using a water jug I found on one of the portages, the one benefit of finding some misguided camper's gear being left behind on a portage. Thankfully, that night I hadn't drunk as much tea before bed as Andy. He woke me up to ask if he could borrow mine. He'd already filled his.

Packing up in the morning was brutal. Andy unzipped the tent fly to retrieve his boots so he could lace them up inside the tent. The mosquitoes used his hikers as a trojan horse and, once inside, attacked us in hordes.

We splashed more bug repellent on us than a gigolo does cologne and went out to the tent to meet our fate. Breakfast was a quick coffee and a hard granola bar. We rolled the tent up in haste, made a swift and unspeakable visit to the thunderbox — where we donated much blood — and then headed downriver, praying for a breeze.

Not surprisingly, Andy's appreciation of the Nipissing increased along the middle section of the river. Here massive old-growth pines root along the banks and cast their shadows on the river. It felt like being in a cathedral.

The rich history of the river revealed itself along the way. We stopped at a couple of spots to find remnants of past lumber camps. At one time, this was a bustling place. Logging began in the Algonquin region in 1830 and the last log drive on the Nipissing was in 1945.

The first huts built by loggers along the Nipissing were crude and simple. Huts were built in three days, measuring 40 square feet (eight square meters) and six logs high. Pine logs were used and moss was stuffed into cracks from the outside and mud from the inside. There were no windows. The only light penetrating the damp living space was from the opening in the roof for a central fireplace. Bunks were lined up along the wall and a separate living area was given to the foreman, cook and clerk. A stable for the horses and a storehouse were built in similar fashion.

Things improved in time. Separate shanties were built for sleeping and cooking, and stoves were added. The cook supplemented the regular diet of bread, beans and pork by adding beef, onions, rice, raisins and dried apples to the menu.

A number of camps were situated along the Nipissing, as it was one of the main rivers used to drive logs. The other main arteries were the Petawawa, Madawaska and Opeongo rivers. Logs were squared, flushed down and rafted over 300 kilometers (186 miles) before being gathered up on the Ottawa River. With each river flushing thousands of logs, hundreds of thousands of logs would cover the Ottawa River from bank to bank. The logs were then floated down to Quebec City and placed on outgoing sailing ships bound for European ship-building yards.

Spring meltwater was used to push the logs downstream. These massive sections of squared timber would speed down the river, just like freighter trucks down a narrow highway. The danger, of course, is that if once one log jammed, the others would pile up behind it. It was the log driver's job to untangle the bundle of giant sticks without being crushed or drowned. Many failed, and many crosses are found along the banks of Algonquin's rivers.

The loggers controlled the water during the spring thaw by building a series of dams and chutes. Dams held back the water to be used when needed, and chutes were used to direct the logs around impassable obstacles, like rapids. These structures remain, and Andy and I spent time checking them out. The lumber camps were more challenging to locate, marked only by an open patch of grass mixed in with raspberry and wild rose bushes. Many artifacts had been picked clean from collectors. One particular place we explored is just upstream of High Falls and used as a POW camp for German soldiers during World War II.

The prisoners were brought in to work at the lumber camps due to the shortage of manpower during the war. The Nipissing camp was made up of German Merchant Mariners, most of who fought in Northern Africa and India. They were guarded by WWI veterans, armed with 303 rifles.

The records show a few escape attempts. One made it to a hotel in Windsor, in the far reaches of southern Ontario, before being captured. Another man went missing, only to be discovered by the guards the next morning. It wasn't an escape attempt — the prisoner had just gotten lost in the woods and prayed the guards would find him before morning. A father and son escaped and remained in Canada after the war. They turned themselves in seven years later. The RCMP (Royal Canadian Mounted Police) let them go, and they soon became Canadian citizens.

It took 70 years to cut Algonquin's giant pines down with axe and saw. The loggers then switched to hardwood and by 1920 a significant industry was built on Algonquin's maple and yellow birch. Trains replaced horses and river drives. Then came roads.

Logging continues today in Algonquin. It's the only provincial park that still allows logging, which continues to be a source of controversy between local lumbermen and conservationists. In the 1950s, the tension grew until a series of harvest limits were imposed. In 1968, the Wildlands League, a conservationist group, was formed. Their purpose was to stop logging in Algonquin completely. The lumber companies labeled the organization a bunch of "canoeing elitists" from the city who should have no say in what happens in the park.

Tensions continued, and in 1974 the Algonquin Master Plan was drafted to appease both sides. The report attempted to separate logging activities and recreational uses. New protective zones were created to help preserve Algonquin's key ecological areas. The Algonquin Forestry Authority was formed, placing the provincial government in control of logging in the park, rather than a patchwork of 20 different private companies that, until then, had run the show.

Even with the limitations, 80 percent of the park could be logged. Wildlands League had lost their battle — but not the war. In 2012, a revised Management Plan removed over 96,000 hectares of the park from logging activity. In 2014, Ontario's Environmental Commissioner released a report that included advisement for a complete logging ban in Ontario's flagship park. He stated that "ecological integrity should be the top priority for managing and operating all parks." Maybe the war is about to end. At present, more than 300 people work at cutting and managing the park's trees and more than 3,000 are employed by local mills. Sales of forest products were over $20 million in 2017.

15
Stolen Whisky

"Every bad situation is a blues song waiting to happen."
AMY WINEHOUSE

It took us another two days to paddle the remaining portion of the Nipissing. The river goes straight across Algonquin. The further along it you get, the wider the banks and the more continuously twisting a waterway it becomes. The mosquitoes remained problematic and by the end, we both just wanted to be done with the river. I cast a line for trout only twice in two days, a real sin for an avid angler like myself. I just couldn't handle swatting at the buzzing bugs around me long enough to pitch a fly. Andy and I rejoiced the moment we exited the river and paddled out onto the expanse of Cedar Lake. Finally, a stiff breeze knocked the bugs down so we could gain our sanity.

Be warned — Cedar Lake is large and has been the unfortunate location of several drownings over the years. Dangerous winds can whip up waves in minutes, as we experienced on our crossing. Andy and I were glad to make it to the Brent dock without capsizing.

The town of Brent isn't much of a town anymore. It housed several lumber camps in the late 19th and early 20th century. It got busier when the Canadian National Railway made it a regular stopover between Ottawa and Capreol. The town was named after Brentwood, England, the home of Robert M. Horne-Payne, director of the Canadian Northern Railway. In 1995 the entire rail line was closed as its revenue wasn't keeping up with the operating costs.

Along with the railway's departure, so too went electricity, making all the locals to leave town. Now it's a seasonal place, offering a campground and supply store. A restored ranger's cabin, built in 1932, can also be reserved by park users.

We picked up our second food drop at Brent's Algonquin Outfitters store, run by Jake Pigeon, an Algonquin legend who recently received the 2013 Director's Award from Algonquin Park officials. He hadn't changed much since last time I paddled through and stopped for a visit. Jake supports promoting the more secluded northern areas of Algonquin but is hesitant to encourage inexperienced trippers to explore here. He's right — this area is not for the timid. The lakes are big, the portages are rough, and the park's remoteness is intensified.

In our resupply, a one-liter Platypus bag of Black Grouse blended malt was missing. It quickly became the talk of the town and locals wanted to come to our rescue. Larry, a park staff employee, offered to give us a replacement, and so did some members from a road construction crew. Even a random boater offered us a bottle.

Unknown to Andy and me, we had gained some celebrity status after being interviewed on CBC Radio a few times during the trip by way of a satellite phone. I was posting Facebook updates by way of a wireless router linked to my satellite phone. We could send but couldn't receive so we had no idea that the Facebook page had gained over 11,000 visits. By the time we finished the trip, Andy and I were minor rockstars on social media. Cool!

I announced the stolen whisky on the radio and social media. As a result, in addition to the Brent locals offering us replacement booze, several social media friends canoed into the park to deliver us whisky. A number of portages after leaving Brent, we came across a note posted on a tree encouraging us on our trip, with a flask of whisky stashed below. All these kindred spirits helping out their fellow paddlers sure cheered us up.

I later discovered that our whisky had been taken from our resupply cache by someone who didn't agree with the non-traditional way we were conducting our trip. This person was of the opinion that paddlers should complete the Meanest Link the "right" way — with a cedar-canvas canoe, not a lightweight model as thin as a potato chip. In this person's view, the Meanest Link is also supposed to be completed as quickly as possible and without food cached along the way. Our opinion differed, obviously.

Andy and I were two 50-year-old paddlers who welcomed a light canoe, cherished our food caches, and couldn't care less about how fast we paddled the route. Our naysayer thought of us as the devil. He even labeled me "Lucifer of Algonquin" in a private email. Many more people disagreed, and the whisky deliveries continued. By the time we reached the next food cache, we'd found enough stashed booze to last us a year in the bush.

16
Breaking Park Rules

"Learn the rules like a pro, so you can break them like an artist."
PABLO PICASSO

On our ninth day out we found ourselves paddling in the park's northeastern corner and heading to the south end of the colossal Cedar Lake. It was the Saturday of the July long weekend and even though Andy and I had a camping permit for the lake we couldn't find any of the 30 campsites unoccupied. What to do?

Crowds hadn't been an issue on the route so far, so we weren't accustomed to searching for a site. It was after 8 p.m. and getting dark. So we broke the rules and made a bush camp, making sure to leave no trace. Not the best choice, but the only one that seemed feasible at the time.

The stiff breeze across Cedar Lake finally knocked the bugs down a bit on the small island we'd illegally set up on. We even slept directly in the bug shelter. Andy and I got cozy watching the sunset across the water, and after a late dinner we curled up in our sleeping bags, protected only by a thin veil of black see-through mesh. Of course, the idea of spending the night in the shelter rather than pitching the tent up might also have been generated by pouring ourselves an extra whisky or two to celebrate getting past our half-way point. We didn't get tipsy, just too comfortable to move.

We woke up extra early and retreated from our illegal overnight site before a park warden spotted us. We had a good defense in case we got caught; still, it's against the rules of Algonquin to camp on a non-designated site.

We continued paddling downriver, heading east, but now on the much bigger Petawawa River. There was a huge difference between the Petawawa and the Nipissing. Red pine dominated the riverbanks instead of white, steep granite took over the shoreline, and the portages avoided much bigger stretches of whitewater. We also saw more paddlers. We had met only two on the lower Nipissing — a father and daughter on a fishing trip — but came across a couple dozen on the Petawawa. Many were whitewater paddlers heading down the full length of the river, equipped with banana-shaped boats and adorned with helmets, GoPros and brightly-colored PFDs.

It was nice to see more people in the park. I like people and consider myself a social person. Sure, there are times on a canoe trip when I find it awkward to run into other paddlers. After all, I like seeking out remote areas where no one else goes. But you can gather lots of wisdom from other paddlers.

A few years back I launched a new film called *Wilderness Quest* and one of the first questions from the media was, "What was the most inspiring thing that happened to you while filming and canoeing around the remote interior of Quetico Provincial Park?" Oddly, I blurted out, "Meeting people out there."

My answer surprised the journalist. I'm sure he was expecting me to offer some poetic views on solitude and seclusion. The film is called *Wilderness Quest*, after all and has all the standard scenes of loons, sunsets, nasty portages, bugs, scary thunderstorms, beautiful landscapes and moonlit paddles. However, in retrospect, it was the grab bag of paddlers I met out on the portages and campsites who motivated me the most. Sharing with me their diverse reasons about why they love the wilderness is what made the project truly worthwhile.

Some of the more memorable characters included two stoner chicks who proudly showed off the biceps they had gained from portaging; an interior maintenance crew boss who expressed his appreciation of wilderness travel with quotes from Thoreau; and a government minister from Germany — wearing a pair of lederhosen — who recounted real moments of spiritual utopia. Then there was the slothful teenager conveying how he had his best nap ever while canoeing in Quetico; the deep-thinking philosopher who wished for the simpler life of being a tree or a bird; and the retired dentist who loathed seeing anyone while out on trip — especially a film crew.

The most inspiring interview was with a middle-aged couple I met after a very long day. The film crew was exhausted and needed a break, but I felt we should talk to the couple. So I offered to carry their canoe across the portage while producer Kip Spidell did the interview.

When I returned, everyone was in tears. The woman had shared her story of her fight with cancer. She and her husband were using this wilderness canoe trip as a chance to re-evaluate their lives. To them, the trip was like starting on a clean page, a reminder of how fleeting our time is — and how they wanted to to spend more of it in wilderness areas.

Like many people, I suffer from an inability to articulate the sense of well-being I feel when spending time in the wilderness. But the candor and comments of the Quetico paddlers gave voice to these feelings. For that, I'm glad I met so many people out there on my wilderness quest.

17
History Along the Petawawa

"The importance of the river cannot be overstated in the history of the country, or the development of the nation."
MAURICE HINCHEY

The Algonquin Natives, descendants of the Archaic and Woodland people, traveled the Petawawa extensively before European contact. The majority of Native artifacts discovered in Algonquin were found along the river, with a total of 170 archeological sites investigated. The oldest artifacts are stone tools from the ancient Laurentian Archaic period, some 8,000 years ago.

The French explorer Samuel de Champlain was the first to record the Algonquin people. He met a group along the St. Lawrence River in 1603 while they gathered with their allies to celebrate their victory against the raiding Iroquois.

Algonquin groups migrated from the Ottawa Valley to the upper Petawawa in autumn to catch trout and eel. This might be why some experts believe the term *"Algonquin"* means *"at the place of spearing fishes and eels from the bow of a canoe."* Another translation is *"they are our relatives."* To me the second makes sense, since the Algonquin were so widespread, being almost completely nomadic (hunting, fishing and trapping) and mixed in with many other Native groups. In fact, the first language a fur trader was told to learn before heading into the interior was the Algonquin's, because so many other Native groups recognized it.

The number of Algonquins in the Ottawa Valley dwindled extensively after the Europeans arrived in the search for fur and settlement. Vast numbers died of smallpox and measles, and even more from Iroquois raiding parties, wanting control over trapping grounds and travel routes.

The Algonquin partnered with French fur traders, who gave guns to Christian converts. The Dutch and English fur traders gave them to any Iroquois that asked. By 1642, the Algonquin were running for their lives, escaping north and west. By 1650, the only Algonquin that remained on their former lands were a scattering of families hidden along the small tributaries of the Ottawa River, most likely the rivers now inside Algonquin Park.

When the French lost against the British in 1760, it was negotiated between the two that the Algonquin, allies of the French, were not to be "molested on any pretense whatsoever." Algonquins started to return to their original hunting grounds, and some even helped the British defeat the Americans at the Battle of Chateauguay during the War of 1812. There are now 11,000 people claiming Algonquin heritage, and theirs is the largest land claim in Ontario.

Naming Algonquin Park after the Algonquin Natives was suggested by Alexander Kirkwood, a government land surveyor, who proposed that the park be formed in the first place. "In adapting the word, we perpetuate the name of one of the greatest Indian nations that has inhabited the North America continent," he wrote.

It wasn't until after the War of 1812 that Europeans started accurately mapping parts of Algonquin Park, including the Petawawa. The British were worried about moving soldiers and supplies too close to the Americans along the St. Lawrence and on the Great Lakes. Engineers were sent out to look for an alternative route to construct a canal — somewhere between Georgian Bay and the Ottawa River — where a canal could be constructed.

Lieutenant James Catty of the Royal Engineers was the first to go looking, in 1818. The closest he got to Algonquin was its "panhandle" on the southern border. Henry Briscoe, another Lieutenant of the Royal Engineers and veteran of the War of 1812, went next in 1826. Led by a half-Iroquois guide, he traveled the Severn, Muskoka, Oxtongue and

Madawaska rivers. Low water levels on the Madawaska sent him north for an alternative route to the Ottawa River, through a chain of Algonquin lakes to Cedar Lake and down the Petawawa. He considered the entire route to be a terrible place to build a canal.

Lieutenant Briscoe and Lieutenant William Greenwood followed in 1827, but took the Madawaska to the Ottawa and echoed Briscoe's report about the rugged landscape and the many falls and rapids. The same year, Lieutenant John Walpole and surveyor James Chewett gave Catty's old route another try and reported it unsuitable.

Alexander Shirreff, who had done surveys for the Rideau Canal, traveled the Petawawa twice in 1829, also looking for a route to build a canal. He entered at Radiant Lake by a series of lakes and portages and went south across Algonquin after Cedar Lake, following a map given to him by Constant Pennaissez, son of an Algonquin Chief. He described the land they traveled through in more positive terms than other Europeans had narrated in their journals. "The scenery is of the most pleasant and inviting nature…" However, beyond his detailed descriptions of massive white pine and gigantic lake trout, he also noted it was a horrible place to build a canal.

The famed explorer and mapmaker of Canada's west, David Thompson, was taken out of retirement in 1837 to look for a canal route as well. He kept away from the Petawawa River and used the Muskoka, Oxtongue and Madawaska rivers to reach the Ottawa. He reported to the Provincial Secretary that his survey was an utter failure.

No canal was ever built.

18
Bill Mason's River

"When you look at the face of Canada and study the geography carefully, you come away with the feeling that God could have designed the canoe first and then set about to conceive a land in which it could flourish."

BILL MASON

If it weren't for the development of the park, the Petawawa River would have certainly been dammed for hydropower. The river drops 250 meters (820 feet) along its course, and a good portion of that happens to be the middle section, just before and just after it enters Cedar Lake.

After Cedar, the river flushes into Radiant Lake, a bowl-shaped lake complete with sandy beaches and crosses marking the graves of long-dead log drivers.

A haze of smoke from distant forest fires blocked most of our view crossing Radiant. And what a shame — Radiant is beautiful. It's like no other lake in the park. Its shallow sand beaches make up the majority of the shoreline, and more bass and walleye lurk in the waters than trout.

It was a little unnerving paddling through the smoke. We later found out the fires were a few hundred kilometers away in northern Quebec; still, we found the smoke was thick enough to make breathing difficult. It was one of the few times I felt vulnerable in the wilderness.

We hugged the shoreline and felt our way along to the southwestern section of the lake where the Petawawa drains. We were surprised to hear a motorboat buzzing across Radiant. Andy and I had forgotten that motors of 10 horsepower or less are allowed on the lake. There are a few rustic cottages on the northwestern shoreline. The owners arrive by either an old road or by taking an ATV down the abandoned Canadian National Railway line.

I felt this intrusion of machines and men didn't take away from our wild surroundings at all. Radiant Lake is far less busy now than it was in the past. The Canadian National Railway ran through Algonquin from 1915 to 1995. When the railway was running, this was a primary access point for canoeists entering the park. The authors of the well-known Algonquin book *The Incomplete Anglers* began their trek across the park by jumping off the train here. The classic book, written by John D. Robins and published in 1943, tells of two anglers on a canoe fishing trip in Algonquin in the mid-1930s.

The train station was west of where the Petawawa River flushes into the lake. The park's office, run by legendary park ranger Zeph Nadon, known for his extensive winter treks across the park, was located on the opposite corner of the lake.

In 1847 J. MacDonell, the original land surveyor of the Algonquin region, recorded numerous Native camps of Algonquin on Radiant Lake (then called Trout Lake) when he stopped to purchase a canoe. It was during the logging era, however, that Radiant Lake saw the most traffic. Various lumber companies, including J.R. Booth, Gillies Bros. and Harris and Bronson Co., occupied the lake, especially in the 1930s. A large depot farm was constructed along the west shore and a steam-powered tug boomed logs into the bay of the North River.

Andy and I took time out to visit the loggers' gravesites noted on our park map.

The graves themselves aren't easy to find, but we found the memorial plaque easily enough. It was located on the southeast corner of the lake, placed on a large boulder up from a beach. The plaque states, "In this enclosure are buried the bodies of more than 20 rivermen drowned in the nearby waters before 1916 when the railway was completed."

From the plaque, we followed a faint trail to the east through an alder thicket that ends at the Bissett Creek/Radiant Road. According to the information I had gathered from Donald L. Lloyd's book, *Canoeing Algonquin Park*, an even fainter trail to the left of the plaque will lead to a wooden staff that marks the whereabouts of a single wooden cross held together with binder twine. Andy and I found the side trail, but no evidence of a wooden staff or graves. I'm guessing too much time has passed and any traces at this point have blended in with the forest.

The Petawawa was Bill Mason's favorite river. He was a filmmaker, author and conservationist. During the late '70s and early '80s he was a legend in the canoe world. Now, not so much.

Music died for Don McLean when the rock legend, Buddy Holly, died in a plane crash in 1959. The day the music died for me was the moment my class of college students got bored two minutes into Bill Mason's 1985 film *Waterwalker*. They were a group from my outdoor leadership class, and I thought it was prudent to show them this classic canoe flick.

The eyeballs started to roll during the synthesized beats of Bruce Cockburn's opening song. Then a few students began snoozing while Mason drifted through a beautiful early morning fog. By the time the stunning scene appears of Mason painting on a rock ledge overlooking Lake Superior and there wasn't a single "wow," I knew I'd lost them.

I grew up watching *Waterwalker*. I still watch it, over and over again — all 86 minutes. It gets me through the long winters and prolonged spring thaws. The film has inspired a generation to get outdoors, and it does that by taking you on a wilderness journey in Mason's iconic red canoe.

Canoe trips are about peace and solitude. But they're also about getting in touch with your true self. It's a simple lifestyle. "The path of the paddle can be a means of getting things back to their original perspective," Mason said famously.

Throughout the film, Mason's squeaky, non-preachy voice underlines important issues on environmental conservation and indigenous philosophy. It even touches on personal spirituality and how it connects to the natural world.

Desensitized to danger by waterfall-hucking Red Bull athletes, not one of my students even flinched when Mason dumped his canoe in freezing water and came close to death. It was obvious the students weren't connecting with Mason's canonical work. Maybe they couldn't. The symbolic red Prospector canoe set amongst the vast wilderness has been replaced by campgrounds providing free WiFi.

Mason made us dream. He inspired us to go out canoeing as he did. We liked his films not just because we liked him — we wanted to be him. We wanted to be free, sit in that red canoe and roam the wilderness waterways for an extended periods of time.

Mason wasn't the only one who loved paddling the Petawawa River. Former Prime Minister Pierre Elliott Trudeau loved canoe-tripping down the Petawawa. He wrote about the nobility of soul and spirit of such a river trip. "What sets a canoeing expedition apart is that it purifies you more rapidly and inescapably than any other. Travel a thousand miles by train and you are a brute; pedal five hundred on a bicycle and you remain basically a bourgeois; paddle a hundred in a canoe and you are already a child of nature."

Another was Trudeau's friend Blair Fraser, a leading Canadian journalist, editor of *Maclean's* magazine, and a member of the group of diplomats and journalists who were dubbed The Voyageurs. Each year they would gather and retrace a historic Canada fur trade route by canoe. In the group were legendary paddlers and conservationists Eric Morse and Sigurd Olson.

One of The Voyageurs' favorite spring practice runs before embarking on trips further north was the Petawawa. Sadly, on May 12, 1968, Blair Fraser drowned on a rapid called Rollway. He didn't set out to flush down the long set of whitewater. Supposedly, he was busy conversing about the Vietnam War with his canoe partner, Elliot Rodger, a retired Major-General of the Canadian Forces, and missed the take-out for the portage. Their canoe dumped not far into the run. His partner survived, but Fraser hit his head on a rock and drowned.

In September of that year, Blair Fraser's fellow Voyageurs gained permission from Algonquin park officials and gathered at the rapid to erect a commemorative cross, reading "In Memory of Blair Fraser, 1909-1968."

The cross remained on the riverbank for 40 years. Then, in 2008 someone — a vigilante-style activist who was opposed to any memorial placed in a wilderness setting — cut it down with a hacksaw.

AN EPIC CANOE JOURNEY

The perpetrator sent out letters to various people, including the park superintendent and me. It had no signature, no return address and rambled on about why monuments have no right to be in wild places.

> *"The Rollway cross was thoughtfully removed, as was its spawn: a plaque screwed to a tree in the midst of a falls campsite, and a large freshly carved marble plaque from the "Gourmet Paddlers" on behalf of one of their kin, prominently urethane foamed to a rock at a popular scenic location and adorned with a toy plastic canoe. Make peace with your own mortality, park your sense of self-importance and recognize immortality graffiti where you see it. Meanwhile, a small, frail, anonymous memento hides in a special spot requiring days of tripping and hiking to reach, on behalf of someone's dying wish. You can appreciate the difference, There is more traffic in the park these days. Why not direct your attention to the Industrial Minerals Graphite Mine coming to life just north of Travers?"*
>
> PASSING THROUGH

The way it was written made me think "Passing Through" was dealing with some extreme emotional disorder and his personal demons had made him a tad unhinged. It made me uncomfortable, even nervous, that he'd put me on his hit list.

Minutes after I read the letter, the phone rang. It was my daughter's school. She had her first day of kindergarten and the principal, with a calm, soft voice, said: "Now, please don't panic, but we can't seem to locate your daughter."

Of course, I panicked. What father wouldn't?

It turned out that my daughter had been put on the wrong bus at the end of the school day and was found at another school down the road. The incident was a terrifying moment I'll never forget, but it had nothing to do with the letter mailed to me. It was just bad timing. Of course, I didn't know that at the time. My anxiety level peaked, and I was left second-guessing doing anything about the act of vandalism. I took the pusillanimous approach and handed the letter over to my good friend James Raffan, the past executive director of the Canadian Canoe Museum.

He got the word out about the missing cross, and it caused a great deal of debate amongst park users. Some simply wanted to know who this chump was and whether or not the law would punish him. Others agreed with the guy's illegal actions, saying they wished they'd thought of it first. Some questioned the difference between plaques. There are plaques that celebrate Algonquin artists like Tom Thomson on Canoe Lake, and outstanding park rangers, like F.X. Robichaud and Tom Wattie on North Tea Lake. There's also a memorial screwed into the granite on the central island of Happy Isle Lake, overlooking the final campsite of father and son Van Ness Delamater and Van Ness Delamater Jr., who drowned during a violent storm in 1931. Do ordinary canoeists compare to noteworthy artists and park rangers?

The one canoeist who was enraged by the "ignorant act of an ignorant person" was Michael Peake, publisher of *Che-Mun: The Journal of Canadian Wilderness Canoeing*. He's spent a good portion of his life retracing, documenting and adoring The Voyageurs, and Blair Fraser was one of his favorite members. Peake said "To that Memorial Monkey-Wrencher who views any wilderness memorial with disgust — wake up and smell the history."

Blair Fraser was an extraordinary person and was highly respected for the love he had for Canada's wild places. This is why Peake was so annoyed with the agitator. He believed that if you desecrate a memorial, you undermine the ideas and people it stands for.

I share similar views with Peake, but I waited a few years before I broke my cowardly silence to express them publicly. Author and Algonquin canoeing devotee Roy MacGregor quoted my feelings in his book, *Canoe Country*:

> "When I come to a memorial in the woods, I always feel a sense of empathy to the one who died and the family they've left behind. More strongly, however, I sense the connection the deceased had with nature and how they felt about being in the wilderness. By placing the memorial — beyond helping the ones closest to the deceased deal with the death in a remote and uncommon setting — it gives a strong message to strangers passing by. It reminds them of how we all are a part of nature, not detached from it."

It was what became of the cross that really pissed a lot of paddlers off. The bronze shrine was found in 2012 by a group of canoeists who were traveling down the Petawawa in low water. They saw it shimmering on the river bottom near where it was once cemented upright. The vandalizer had just cut the metal off its perch and tossed it in the river, just as a litterer might throw a bag of garbage out the window of a moving car on some backcountry road. It was still in the park, but hidden from the view of paddlers passing by.

Friends and family returned to the site with the park officials' permission and re-anchored the cross back to its resting place along the Petawawa. No longer was it hidden in the depths of the raging rapids that killed Blair. The memorial now stands as a reminder of the dangers of paddling a wild river and the joys that one paddler once felt being there.

19
Trout on the Crow River

*"Things fishermen know about trout aren't facts,
but articles of faith."*
JOHN GIERACH

Andy and I were able to reach where the Crow River plunges into the Petawawa River before making camp. The cascade is called Blueberry Falls, and even though the campsite wasn't the best, the scenery around us was spectacular.

The Crow River was our fourth river on route. We were leaving the Petawawa River and moving east, deeper into the interior of the park. It was flowing the wrong way for the direction of our travel, but it didn't matter much. The river has 14 portages, adding up to over four kilometers (2.5 miles), so we walked more than paddled.

The difficulty of the Crow didn't faze us. Maybe we were in better shape at this point in the trip or perhaps because the Crow River is a true gem of Algonquin. The river is legendary both for its scenery and for its incredible brook trout fishing. Nine casts during lunch gave me eight brook trout, each averaging a couple of pounds. It was like reliving the book, *The Incomplete Angler*. How incredible to catch just as many fish as had the book's author, John D. Robins, proof that a long portage might be the only thing that can really keep a wilderness area wild.

I've had my fair share of long, steep and nasty portages. They're never enjoyable, and it's the sweet moment of spotting the sparkle of shimmering water in the distance that makes the abuse we endure worth it. The more you do, however, the more you learn to grin and bear it. And there is an art to it.

Make sure to perfect your dance. Don't let the canoe take the lead. You don't want a gracious disco move turning into an awkward looking Irish jig. Trouble usually starts when trying to slam through overgrowth and being violently thrown backward by the strength of the branches and weight of the boat. Remember, being knee-deep in mud, and balancing the canoe like an oversized cake topper is no time to perfect a pirouette.

If you fall, fall with dignity. Eventually, the slippery rocks and exposed roots will induce a series of unbalanced teetering, which will result in a nasty fall. I only rate it as a stumble unless the canoe comes crashing down on my head. In any case, a true fellow camper won't judge you, unless you turtle.

What gets each canoeist to the other side of a portage varies. Some treat themselves to snacks from the candy bag. Others go into a dreamscape of past dates that went well, movies worth seeing a second time, dirty tricks to play on the boss, and — my favorite — portages I've had to endure that were worse than the one I'm on.

People think about the things they endure happening back at home — like traffic jams and noise pollution — to justify the pain of the portage and make it seem not so bad after all. Many paddlers hum monotonous show tunes or songs they heard on the radio on the drive to the put-in to pass the time away. The Proclaimers' "I'm Gonna Be (500 Miles)" tops my list; so does "Dancing Queen" by ABBA, Harry Chapin's "Cat's in the Cradle," and John Denver's "Poems, Prayers and Promises." On one nightmarish 27-day solo trip, I couldn't get Aqua's "Barbie Girl" out of my head.

At the beginning of a trip I daydream of the monster fish, picturesque campsites and the peaceful solitude I know I'll find deep in the interior. Near the end of the journey, it's the thought of a cold beer and roadside junk food quickening my pace across the trail. Ultimately, what gets most of us to the other side — no matter when and where — is the fact that the portage, nasty or not, is the only thing protecting the solitude of the place we're heading.

It's pretty much a guarantee that whoever suffers the greatest will be enriched the most. A portage with a few steep inclines and a squishy spruce bog will have no crowd on the other side. If you do stumble across another paddler — ideally, not when you're belting out "Come on Barbie, let's go party!" — rest assured, they'll be just as passionately in love with the pain and pleasure of portaging as you are.

20
A Toast to Swifty on Lake Lavielle

*"Wherever there is a channel for water,
there is a road for the canoe."*
HENRY DAVID THOREAU

Andy and I kept three small brook trout for dinner when we reached Lake Lavielle, another gem of Algonquin. We stayed on Bill Swift Senior's favorite campsite, which was the large island along the eastern shore. It's a tradition for paddlers taking on the Meanest Link to stay here and toast "Swifty," whom the route honors.

Swift and Dave Waiman, a former park ranger, opened up Algonquin Outfitters on Oxtongue Lake back in 1961. A fleet of 40 cedar-canvas Chestnut canoes was shipped to the store by train from the factory out in Fredericton, New Brunswick. Thirty years later the business expanded to Brent, Opeongo and Huntsville.

Swifty's love affair with Algonquin began in the late 1930s, when he was a camper at Camp Pathfinder on Source Lake. He later became a camp counselor and then bought the camp, owning it through the 1960s and early 1970s. He was a busy man as a founding board member of the Canadian Recreational Canoeing Association, the Algonquin Wildland League and longtime board member of the Northern Ontario Tourist Outfitters Association. His two sons helped out. Rich ran the outfitting business and Bill developed Swift Canoes. In 1997, the Friends of Algonquin Park awarded Bill Swift Sr. the prestigious Director's Award. Two years later he died of a heart attack, leaving memories of laughter, ambition and a deep cherished love for Algonquin.

I wonder what the outspoken Bill Swift Sr. would have said about the changes to his beloved Lake Lavielle and neighboring Dickson Lake. For the last few years, blue-green algae has closed a portion of Lavielle and all of Dickson to camping. The lakes have been poisoned by naturally occurring microscopic organisms called cyanobacteria. Some claim the bloom is caused by cormorants pooping too much in the water; others say global warming, and others are just baffled.

Both lakes are considered absolute treasures — deep, cool, clear and well-oxygenated bodies of water teaming with trout. Dickson Lake brook trout is the strain used to stock other Algonquin Park lakes. Some worry that the algae bloom could deplete enough oxygen content to kill off the trout.

To many park users, trout fishing defines Algonquin. Hundreds of anglers dream of the yearly ritual of heading out on opening day of the season, paddling and portaging deep into the interior in search of trophy square tails and fat lakers, praying the ice has left the lakes and the black flies have yet to hatch. The park's fisheries department has invested lots of time and money in making sure the trout population remains sustainable. The effects of mercury contamination and acidification from acid rain have been researched extensively, as has over-harvesting. And now there's the blue-green algae problem.

Trout are finicky fish. They're slow to grow, late to mature and have low reproductive rates. They also don't get along with other fish, especially during spawning. Perch will take over their food source, and pike can decimate them. Algonquin has the majority of Ontario's naturally reproducing trout lakes, which makes it special. However, only 240 of Algonquin's 1,400 lakes have self-sustaining trout populations. The others need help by re-stocking efforts.

Trout are great indicator species because they're one of the first species to be affected by change. The decline of Algonquin's brook trout and lake trout would herald the death of the park's *raison d'etre*. To me, catching a wild native trout is one of the true symbols of wilderness. Once you've lost this ability, there's no turning back.

Methods to protect the Algonquin trout have varied over the years. Some were grave mistakes: for example, dumping fertilizer and introducing Cisco to some lakes, both which were thought to fatten the fish up and make anglers happier with their catches. Other conservation efforts, such as size limits, banning baitfish and closing a lake off to fishermen for a period, seem to be working. However, the main reason trout still thrive in Algonquin, is that it's still darn difficult to reach the prime interior lakes to try your luck.

And once an Algonquin angler finds his honey hole, he usually takes it to his grave.

To emphasize this sacred fishing spot ideology, consider a debate on social media. Angler and Algonquin regular Mike Borger and his 10-year-old son documented a fishing trip they took in the interior of Algonquin on YouTube. They found a hot spot, visited on a previous trip by Bolger. The video shows him and his son catching six five-pound brook trout and countless others weighing between three and four pounds.

Father and son captured a memory that would last forever then uploaded it to YouTube. Borger received more than 200 requests asking for the lake's location. He politely declined to reveal it.

Out of the pumpkin patch always comes a sour lemon. One viewer wanted to know where the honey hole was so badly that he made a Freedom of Information request to the provincial government to find out where Borger was fishing. The viewer asked the government to see Borger's camping permit, which would uncover the lakes traveled and fished.

After consideration, the Ministry told Borger they would not confirm or deny the existence of his permit to the person pursuing it. The Ministry must be staffed with trout anglers themselves. But the nosy YouTube viewer appealed — twice. Ultimately, after the second appeal, the request was denied.

I'd never thought I'd see the day when this sort of thing would happen amongst our creed. My dad would be rolling in his grave at it all. Trout fishing was my religion growing up. My dad introduced me to wilderness travel by taking me fishing — and it was always for trout.

He brought me up in a traditional sense — to always work hard, be honest to others and know that the only valid fish to catch is a trout. Why? Because trout are hard to catch. You need to work extra hard to find them, and you need incredible skill to catch one. They represent, at least to me, the essence of true wilderness values. The moment water becomes tainted or a road creates easy access, the trout disappear, along with what they represent.

As a child, the act of fishing itself was my doorway to time spent outdoors. Even at a young age, I knew catching the fish was anticlimactic. The exciting part was trying to catch a fish, and the more difficult the species was to catch the more robust the memory of the event and the more respect you gave to the species itself. Trout was always the unyielding species to angle for.

My early years were spent just dangling a worm in a local creek. It wasn't until my pre-teens that my father took me to a bonafide trout stream with deep pools and rapids to cast a small spinner. It was on my 16th birthday, and my father gave me a fly rod. By my early twenties, it was rare I'd replace the fly with a worm or spinner.

Fly fishing is a lot like golf. The more you try, the worse you get. But the moment you give up and don't care whether you strike the darn ball or not, you get a hole-in-one. By then, you've figured out the groove. Timing and feel are the two crucial elements. The line is flung behind you, and if you abruptly stop the rod at the appropriate moment, it just feels right. The line straightens out and you sense a slight tug of the tension which travels back down to your grip. It's at this particular moment that you initiate your forward cast, making the fly land on the water as nature intended it.

I perpetuated this ideology with my nephew, Todd, while he was growing up. The poor guy. I used to tease him mercilessly when we'd gather during family holidays and share fishing tales. He'd share stories of catching big bass or pike, and I'd always rudely interrupted him halfway through by blurting out, "So, when are you going to catch a real fish — a trout on a fly?"

Years later, I talked about trout fishing with my nephew. It was at my father's funeral. Todd had been away fishing in northern Canada and came home for the service. After spinning a few tales, trying to make light of the situation at hand, Todd asked if he could place something in my father's casket. I said yes, adding my dad would appreciate the gesture.

It was a trout fly Todd gave my father, not a bass jig or pike spoon. We hugged after he had said his prayers, and I whispered, "I guess you went on a real fishing trip while you were in the north." Todd smiled and quite enthusiastically replied, "I caught speckles the size of a champagne bottle, Uncle Kevin. It was fantastic."

21
Opeongo — Algonquin's Largest Lake

"If there is magic on this planet, it is contained in water."
LOREN EISELEY

On the twelfth day of the Meanest Link, we were slow to get moving. The dreaded Dickson-Bonfield portage was waiting for us. Its total distance is just over five kilometers (3.1 miles). Yikes! It called for pouring a second cup of coffee and extra flapjacks.

We soothed ourselves by noting that the day's total portaging distance was actually below our daily average. Seven kilometers of portaging a day was the norm on the Meanest Link. Day 12 had us doing four carries total, one leading into Dickson Lake (where the long portage began) and two more taking us to Opeongo, Algonquin's largest lake. Even still, a five-kilometer portage in one go is intimidating. I've done it several times before and each time I promised myself never to do it again.

Andy and I completed the portage in two hours and 10 minutes. Not a bad time, but not my best. I once completed it in an hour and 40 minutes. I was much younger then, and also had a nuisance bear stalking me most of the way. I had planned to stop every 20 minutes for a break. However, each time I put the canoe down, the bear was standing on the trail behind me, just waiting to rummage through my food pack, so I trotted on.

I had something else to keep me going this time. My marriage was falling apart. My wife and I had been married for 20 years, and together before that for 10. What was happening is something that happens in well over 50 percent of marriages. We disconnected, lacked solid communication and grew anxious around each other.

While I was still madly in love with my wife, I wasn't sure the feeling was reciprocated. For the entire five kilometers of the Dickson-Bonfield portage, I contemplated ways to fix things and alternatives to ending it. Overthinking the issue got me to the end of the portage, but it didn't solve my marriage problems. Two years later she asked for a separation and found someone else. I wandered around dumbfounded for a very long time.

Life is like a portage, I guess.

Two short portages later, Andy and I had the luxury of a boat shuttle waiting to take us across Algonquin's 16-kilometer-long (10-mile-long) Opeongo Lake. We were privileged to have Jerry Shmanda, manager of the Algonquin Outfitter's Opeongo store, do the pick-up. He knows Opeongo Lake inside and out. He also delivered our third and last food drop, which we'd organized through Algonquin Outfitters.

Jerry gave us a personal tour of the historic hotspots on Opeongo, including remnants of fur trading posts, lodges and ranger camps. He also showed us where Opeongo's two fatal bear attacks took place. The first attack happened in 1881. Captain John Dennison, the first and only settler to try and farm in the area, went to check his bear leg-hold traps along the portage leading to Green Lake (now called Happy Isle). His eight-year-old grandson joined him. He assumed the trap was empty, but when the Captain stepped over an immense log, an injured, starving and angry bear was waiting for him. "Go get help!" he called out to his grandson.

The poor kid ran back to the canoe and paddled the 10 kilometers (six miles) to the family farm only to find that his father and uncles were out on a fishing trip. It wasn't until a couple of days later that they went back to the portage and found both the bear and the 82-year-old grandfather dead. The body was returned to the farm and Captain Dennison was buried in a small clearing perched overlooking the east arm of Opeongo.

The gravesite itself created a bit of an Algonquin mystery, an uncertainty that was solved by long-time local historian Michael P. Westner. His daughter, Fiona, is a good friend and co-organizer of the Paddle In The Park contest. She tells the story:

"Using books, and any literature that he could get his hands on, my father spent two years searching the farm for the correct location of Capt. Dennison's grave, and the two massive birch trees said to have been planted upon the deaths of his two grandchildren to mark their little graves. [My father] was convinced the location of the Captain's grave, as described by his collection of various literature, was incorrect.

Just off the portage that connects the north and east arms of Opeongo, on the south side, there was a split rail fenced corral about 20 by 30 feet that the ministry declared was the gravesite. However, back in the day, my father was convinced the ministry was mistaken (the area fenced in seemed much larger than would be needed for a grave and there were no large birch trees around) and took it upon himself to search further.

After a couple of years, his search finally paid off, north of the portage, when he stumbled upon the two great birch trees said to have marked the graves of the Captain's grandchildren. These trees were massive. It took two grown people to put their arms around their trunks. It was an incredible sight to see. He then felt that if he had found the children's graves, which were nowhere near the corral on the portage, that Capt. D's grave would be close as well.

And he was right. Just a short walk thru the bush, in a southeasterly direction, he came across Capt. Dennison's elusive grave. Surrounded by a six- by eight-foot split rail cedar fence, Capt. Dennison lies looking over Opeongo. The only marker, nailed to the front rail at the time when my dad first found it, was a small metal plaque that read: 'At Rest.'

In the course of searching the farm, we even stumbled upon his old boat where the entrance to the farm was, but where the remnants are no longer visible today. During the years that we searched for the elusive graves, we found the remains of their old farm buildings, another rock corral, and even their old well. The old fields were covered with raspberries and grapes, by the time we were on the scene, which the bears relished. We came across more than a few bears in our travels there (which are all stories in themselves!). The unusually high bear population was another scary element to add to the story, especially given the way the Capt. died.

And my dad was truly fascinated by the Dennison story. He would go on for hours about what an incredibly hard life it would have been for the family. The land was so difficult to farm and the conditions so harsh, anything they could farm was never enough to sell to the loggers. There was barely enough for them to survive themselves to make it through the winter. Hunting, trapping, and fishing likely helped them survive. But even still, it was the trapping of a bear that led to the Capt.'s demise.

My dad would tell us the story of Capt. Dennison's death every summer around the campfire. And he would even challenge us young ones to sleep over at the grave site for the night by ourselves — although I will make note that this is something that my father did once attempt to do himself, but chickened out at the last minute!

The Ministry has since made a cement cairn with a new plaque to mark the graves of the Captain and the two grandchildren, as well as a bit of the Dennison story."

Algonquin's second fatal bear attack happened on Opeongo's Bates Island in 1991. Raymond Jakubauskas and Carola Frehe met a horrible fate by way of a healthy eight-year-old male bear weighing 140 kilograms (310 pounds). Carola was the first to be attacked. The bear then turned on Raymond when he attempted to drive the bear off with a paddle. It's believed that both campers died quickly from single blows to the head, a tactic used by bears when preying on moose calves. The bear dragged the bodies farther away from the campsite, feeding on them, then covered them with leaves. The bodies weren't discovered for five days.

Jerry Shmanda, our boat's skipper, was first to arrive at the grisly scene. The couple was late in returning, so he'd gone looking for them. When Jerry arrived on the island, seeing all the gear, boat and even food — an exposed tray of ground beef — just sitting there, he felt there was something not right with the scene. He left and returned with park rangers and police. The bear was found standing over the bodies 125 meters (140 yards) from the campsite and was shot and killed. Park authorities stated it was not a nuisance bear hanging around campgrounds and sniffing through garbage dumps, but a predaceous wild bear. The campers had simply been in the wrong place at the wrong time.

Gord Downie of The Tragically Hip wrote about the event in his song, "The Bear."

> *I waited for more men to come*
> *They docked their boats and cocked their guns*
> *The time for truth and reconciliation's gone*
> *But with my belly full I intended to get*
> *Something done*
>
> *I'm the Islander*
> *Woke up in the dead of spring*
> *More hungry than anything*
> *Islander*

A third fatal bear attack occurred on the east side of the park on May 13, 1978. This one gives me shivers every time I think about it. All attacks are gruesome. This attack was horrific. Three boyhood friends — Billy Rhindress, George Halfkenny and his younger brother Mark — were killed and partially consumed by a predacious male bear. They drove in to fish Forty Mile Creek, then moved on to fish Lone Creek. A few fish were caught near the roadway bridge, but the boys decided to move farther upstream to try their luck — all of them except for their friend Richard Rhindress. He chose to take a nap in the car.

Richard woke around 6:30 p.m. to a darkening sky and a storm brewing. Concerned the others hadn't walked back to the car yet, he called out, walked a section of the river, then drove down the road to search some more. That's when he discovered that his car was leaking gas. He decided to drive out for repairs and come back searching later that night. On the way out, Richard stopped at the Sand Lake Gatehouse to tell a park ranger about the missing boys. At 9:30 p.m. he returned, but couldn't locate Billy, George and Mark.

Police and park staff were informed, and by morning they had helicopters flying a search pattern and troops from the Canadian military from Pembroke searching the woods around Lone Creek. There was still no sign of the young men.

The search concentrated on the west side of Lone Creek. That's where Richard had last seen George fishing. Off a side trail, searchers came upon George's bush jacket, the arms turned inside out, and the back of it smeared with blood. His fishing rod was found downstream, as well a series of distinct bear beds, where a black bear had routinely slept. Mark Halfkenny's glasses were found not far away. So was Billy Rhindress' left shoe, laying close to one very large bear print pressed into the mud.

When the searchers glanced up, they saw a large male black bear, looking right at them; he was perched on top of the three dead boys. The bear faced down the entire group of 30 soldiers. Since all were unarmed, everyone retreated to the road.

Conservation Officer Lorne O'Brien and OPP constable Ray Carson went back armed with a rifle and service revolver. They approached the bodies and caught a glimpse of the bear trying to sneak up from behind them. Three shots from O'Brien's rifle sent the bear falling heavily to the forest floor.

There were many theories as to why the bear attacked. The bear may have thought George was a moose calf while crouched down to fish the trout hole, something it would naturally prey on. George also had four fish stuffed in his pockets. The coroner stated that the two other boys likely met their fates while trying to rescue George.

Even more upsetting about this attack is that bear attacks are extremely rare. The short list of fatalities was placed in the park media to remind campers how infrequent these attacks are. Only two had occurred in the park by then — this one, and the 1881 death on Opeongo Lake. Between those two attacks, millions of people had camped in the park. I understand how it's best to put people at ease when such things happen. If not, phobia creeps in, underlining how vulnerable humans can be out in the woods.

In fact, what experts say is true — you have a much better chance of being killed in an automobile accident on the drive to Algonquin than being mauled by a predacious bear. The real spine-tingling part is how these people died. Being mauled by a bear in the remote wilderness must be a horrible way to go. These were genuinely nice people, lovers of the outdoors, now dead. The death of the boys shocked their community of nearby Petawawa. They were good kids who did good things for their town and school. More than 300 people came to their funeral at St. George's Chapel, and a plaque is still on display in their school noting their shared passion for the wilderness. On it is a quote by Horace Ships reading, "And beyond the last campfire man has faith for friend, and beyond all guidance the courage of God for guides."

To bear proof your camp, I recommend that you hang your food. Hanging food is more about the safety of the bear, with the aim to avoid habituation. It's best to have the rope strung up between two trees, rather than thrown over a single limb. The single limb is easier and faster, though. The trick, however, is not to choose the closest tree to camp. Any local bears probably already know about that tree and might try to retrieve your food simply because they've done it before, maybe successfully. Instead, the moment you get to camp, head out behind the campsite a good 50 meters (55 yards) or more, off the trail, looking for a good tree to hang your food from. If you do it after dinner or at dusk, you're less likely to wander back into the darkened forest far enough to fool the bear.

I'm also paranoid about cooking real greasy bacon in the woods. It's an absolute bear attractant, something I discovered while working with a bear biologist in Algonquin back in the 1980s. We had the job of dealing with a nuisance bear on one of the island campsites on Opeongo Lake. We had to find the bear, shoot it with a dart gun, then relocate it before the drugs wore off. The biologist lured the bear into camp by cooking real bacon over the campfire. The bear sauntered into camp 14 minutes and 23 seconds later.

Remember, those blue camp barrels are not bear-proof barrels. They're a great system to keep everything dry and relatively odor-free, and they can come in handy when traveling in the far north where there are no tall trees to hang your food from. However, in the last few years there have been numerous reports by Algonquin park rangers about campers who have placed their food barrel right beside their tent and been woken up to a bear smashing it to pieces. Remember, if a bear can break into an automobile with one swing of the paw, then a thin plastic barrel is no match for it.

You also shouldn't consider yourself safe from a bear visiting your camp if you pitch your tent on an island. Bears are good swimmers.

On a past trip, my paddling partner at the time, Mike Kipp, pointed out a bear swimming to our island site. I sprinted to my tent and woke my daughter Kyla, telling her to prep for a hasty retreat. In her morning haze, Kyla was distraught — it was her sixth birthday and she was anticipating a breakfast of chocolate cake and the mountain of presents she knew I'd been lugging in my pack the entire trip.

By the time everyone shook off their morning cobwebs, the bear was closing in. I yelled at the bear to turn tail. I shot off a round of bear bangers. Still, it remained determined to make landfall on our island. The bear didn't even blink.

I had an entire arsenal — air horn, bear spray, flares — but, a canoeist to the core, I instinctively reached for my paddle. I beat the paddle against the granite shore and yelled obscenities that I hoped Kyla would forget. An Ojibwa elder and friend, Charlie, had showed me the trick when I visited him at his cabin the year before. He said it mimicked a bull moose banging its antlers on the ground, an animal a bear would question confronting. The bear retreated. Charlie's moose antler trick worked!

The bad news was that the paddle I used was the one Mike had hand-carved for me a few years back. My abuse had split it right down the middle. Mike didn't say much — Mike never really says much. He just solemnly stated, "I guess I'll have to make you a new paddle."

My daughter, with a look of disgust, said, "Dad, I can't believe you scared the bear away from my birthday party!"

22
Getting Comfortable

"You have to leave the city of your comfort and go into the wilderness of your intuition. What you'll discover will be wonderful. What you'll discover is yourself."
ALAN ALDA

By now, camp life had become routine for Andy and me. We set up on a small island at the south end of Opeongo Lake. I set up the tent and unfurled our air mats and sleeping bags while Andy gathered water in the cooking pots. A pleasant breeze off the lake made the bug shelter unnecessary. We poured our pre-dinner dram, unfolded our maps, and discussed our route for the next day. I cooked up dinner, Andy did the dishes and we gathered wood for the evening fire. A second dram was poured, we wrote in our journals and sat back to listen to a loon's call. It was a nice routine. We were comfortable — even when the storm hit.

The clouds moved in fast just around dusk. Then came the distant thunder and flashes of lightning. We set up the tarp over our small fire, switched from whisky to tea, and waited for the rain to pour down. And boy, it did.

According to Parks Canada and the U.S. National Parks Service, getting hit by lightning is one of the number one hazards while roaming around the wilderness. Out of the total amount of campers killed by lightning, more than half were on or near open water.

I guess it's kind of obvious that water and lightning are a natural combination. A lake represents a flat base, and you and your canoe are most likely the only things extending above its flat surface.

Getting to shore the moment you spot a buildup of cumulonimbus clouds signaling that a thunderstorm is coming, is an obviously smart choice. In fact, you're more vulnerable as the storm approaches and departs — if you can hear thunder, you within striking distance.

Most storms are combined with high wind and waves, so making a quick retreat to shore can be more difficult than it sounds. And even when you do reach land, it doesn't mean you're safe. In one major storm in 2006, 20 campers were injured by lightning and falling trees. Jeff Grey, a 26-year-old from Michigan, also died when a tree fell on his tent on Kiosk Lake.

Most lightning victims in Algonquin Park have been injured or killed right at their campsite. Some were hit while they stood on shore, watching the storm.

The majority of victims, however, were struck by a corresponding ground charge while lying asleep in their tents. Lightning is formed as a negative charge from the base of a storm cloud passing over, inducing a positive charge where a negative charge usually is. The positive charge is pulled up and lightning is produced where there's an arc. If you're anywhere near the path of the discharge, you can get zapped.

Weathering an electrical storm on land, however, is still far better than being out on the water. Just make sure you pitch your shelter far away from any mound of high rock or tall trees. Also, the deeper you go into the woods, the better the chance of the lightning hitting another object. Keep as low as possible, but don't lie flat out. Sit on top of a pack or, if you happen to be in the tent when the storm hits, squat on top of your sleeping pad with both feet close together to minimize your exposure to ground current.

Stay put for at least 20 minutes after the storm is over. Lightning can touch down from over two kilometers (1.2 miles) away. Some deaths or injuries have been caused when campers headed to the lakeshore to watch the retreating storm and then got struck by lightning.

To calculate the distance of the storm, count the number of seconds (one Mississippi…two Mississippi…three Mississippi…) between the flash of lightning and the thunder. Then divide by five. You now know how many miles away the storm is.

The reasoning behind this calculation is that sound travels approximately one-fifth of a mile per second. For example, five seconds between flash and crash means the strike is one mile away; 10 seconds means it is two miles away; at 25 seconds it's five miles away and so on.

Andy and I weathered the storm, even reveled in it. We'd been in a lot worse and knew we had the gear and skills to keep safe.

Other paddlers didn't. Out in front of our campsite, we witnessed a youth group being led across an open stretch of water towards a wall of rain, black clouds and countless forks of lightning. It was a foolish move, and it was pure luck they made it across unscathed.

Wilderness skills can't be learned quickly, but many campers I see nowadays don't seem to have the patience — or even the desire — to take the time to do it. Just as watching YouTube videos on how to fix a toilet doesn't make you a trained plumber, the same is true of lighting a fire or erecting a tarp. Practice makes perfect.

This raises another matter: who is responsible for making sure people do know what they're doing when they go into the wilderness? It's an excellent question — something I had a difficult time finding out. The provincial and national parks themselves do little to make ensure everyone is sufficiently skilled before they head out into the interior. They seem to treat it more like a personal responsibility issue.

In my experience, most outfitters take pride in educating the people they help, but some campers don't want the help. I'm not sure how to change that. Governing bodies like Paddle Canada and the Ontario Recreational Canoe and Kayak Association do an excellent job in training people to go on canoe and kayak trips safely, however, training is geared towards those who are already motivated to learn the skills and play safe.

There are some rumblings about making paddling tests mandatory for everyone who goes out canoeing and kayaking, or at least having mandatory educational programs directed towards unskilled paddlers. The province of Ontario has the BoatSmart program, which requires all motorboaters to pass a skills and safety test before getting a license to drive a motorboat. Maybe paddlers should have something similar or maybe that's just another cash grab. Whatever the answer, I grow more frustrated, or even angry, each time I hear about another outdoor mishap in the news.

Algonquin seems to have a couple of deaths by drowning or cold water immersion each year. The more it happens, the more likely it is that regulations will be forced upon those who do play safe. How fair is that? We have to reach the masses, and talk sense with them. Let them know what my mother, who has a strong Scottish disposition, always told me before heading out into the woods: "Dinnea be stupid!"

That's what she would blurt out every time I'd head out on a trip and she still offers me this sage advice. Wear a life jacket, wait until the wind dies down on a lake before crossing it, bring a first-aid kit and know how to use it. Just... dinnea be stupid!

Of course, the worst threat is thinking you have proper skills when you don't. To quote Socrates, "The only true wisdom is in knowing you know nothing." It reminds me of a camper I met in Algonquin a few years back while I was instructing canoe tripping skills at the visitor center. My outspoken Scottish mother would definitely have something to say to him.

It wasn't the shoddy khaki safari suit he was wearing. It wasn't the matching socks that went to his knees. It might have been the rude sexual remarks he made about his wife. What really confirmed this guy was an idiot was the laugh he gave when I suggested he join my canoe tripping workshop.

"Yuk, yuk, yuk," he crowed. It was a demeaning chuckle. "Why bother taking your silly course, hot-shot? I already know how to canoe camp."

Meeting this joker outside a wilderness park's interpretive center was unsettling. I've seen far too many cocky paddlers get into trouble in the woods. In fact, I'd been asked here to provide a skill-building workshop at the park due to an increased number of paddlers lost, injured and even killed while in the Algonquin backcountry. The encounter with this guy left me with a bad feeling.

When I arrived at my campsite at the local campground, I was looking forward to some time to prep for the event the next day. That didn't happen. I heard the unmistakable and grating yuk, yuk, yuk cackle the moment I pulled into my site and cracked the car door open. As soon as I stepped out of the car, he recognized me. He strutted over with a six-pack of Pabst and a folding lawn chair.

As I set up camp, he began telling me about what a great camper he was. He called himself the Master of the Elements. I was in for a horrid night. When he wasn't belittling his wife, he spun tales of outlandish and impossible accomplishments. He drank all of his beer, then mine.

I snuck out of camp before sunrise to get to my workshop. Nine novice campers were looking to advance their skills before their first backcountry canoe trip. The course covered packing, portaging and cooking. Most importantly, we discussed wilderness safety.

While my participants gained insight and new skills, at the end of the day I wondered if I had reached the proper audience. Humble and cautious trippers willing to ask for advice are less likely to find themselves in trouble. In my experience, the cocky ones are more likely to need rescuing.

I was mulling this thought over shortly after leaving the workshop when I came across emergency service vehicles blocking the two-lane Highway 60.

I stopped my car. Off to my right, EMS workers were pulling my campsite neighbor out of a lake.

The Yuk Yuk Man was going to be fine. The paramedics told me that the same man who didn't think he needed some silly course on canoe tripping went for a paddle on a windy day, without a PFD or bailer. He capsized in the cold water, and now the rescue crew was treating the Master of the Elements for hypothermia.

I wasn't surprised that his know-it-all attitude had ended in disaster. Arrogance can be a deadly trait in the wilderness.

23
Portage Etiquette

*"The hardest job kids face today
is learning good manners without seeing any."*

FRED ASTAIRE

Leaving Opeongo Lake and portaging south towards the Madawaska River — the fifth river of our journey around Algonquin Park — was the beginning of the end of our trip. We started seeing more people, more garbage and less wilderness. Our circumstance was laughable at first, especially when taking note of all the bizarre odds and ends left on portages by other paddlers — bottles of men's cologne, spare running shoes, giant jugs of water, a baseball bat, hockey mask, and 23 pairs of socks, just to name a few. Depression set in when we noticed campsites scarred with graffiti, trees hacked away with hatchets, campfires still smoking long after the occupants had left, and garbage strewn about the forest. We even saw human poop floating in the water and counted a total of 11 fire grills left behind at a single campsite.

We knew we were leaving the wilder part of Algonquin when Andy almost got hit by a truck while portaging across the highway that cuts through the park. That made us agitated enough. But while portaging through Whitefish campground, after the highway crossing, we were forced off the portage by a group of young guys approaching on the single-track trail. I was carrying a colossal pack and Andy shouldered his pack and the canoe. This group of campground campers was walking back from a swim, carrying nothing but flip-flops and beach towels. For some reason, they decided they had the right of way and literally sent Andy and I crashing off the trail to get around them.

I lost it with them. When I sternly informed them of their wrongdoing, the group just stood there dumbfounded. One guy even threw back a few nasty curse words, flipped me the bird, and brashly asked where the sign was with a list of all this portage etiquette stuff I was rambling on about.

I left the quarrel muttering about rude people, and how we're doomed as a society. Poor Andy was doomed to listen to my fulminating all afternoon.

What's portage etiquette? Some paddlers just don't know the meaning of it. I've witnessed a camper poop right in the middle of a portage, saw someone pee on a patch of blueberries at the take-out, and watched a youth group block a put-in with their packs and boats and then leave food wrappers, dirty socks and broken lawn chairs strewn in their wake.

Miss Manners would be aghast.

I like to think of a busy portage as a microcosm for the rest of life. In amongst all the nature lovers who want to leave the place a little better than they found it, there's also all the other people. You know the ones. They're the litterers, the ones who wander past complaining, those who come up fast from behind and tailgate. There are others still who are too hurried or self-important even to return a courteous hello.

My biggest pet peeve is oncoming foot traffic that doesn't give a canoe-head the right of way. It feels like being cut-off on the highway, or the victim someone who butts in line at the grocery store. "Excuse me," is the politest thing I can think of to say.

On the portage trail, just as in life, you'll meet jackasses. Just like the guys with the flip-flops.

While many paddlers learn portage etiquette from camp, family members or courses, some can be oblivious to the unwritten rules that many of us cherish. The usual excuse for ignoring protocol? "No one told me!" It reminds me of the old Steve Martin routine, where he says to the judge, "I didn't know armed robbery was illegal. If you told me it was, I wouldn't have done it."

Fortunately, the rules are straightforward. Make way for whoever is carefully carrying an awkward and potentially heavy canoe. Don't poop on the trail — ever. It's gross. Bathrooms breaks should take place 100 meters from the trail and water sources. Finally, leave all your gear neatly off to the side of the access point, and don't leave anything behind when you paddle away.

The golden rule of kindergartners everywhere — to treat others as you want to be treated — also goes a long way. Some might call these rules simple common sense.

On the portage trail, just as in life, you may have to do your best to avoid or reeducate the complainers, the tailgaters, and the poopers. Accept that some paddlers will rush past, others will carry too much, and others won't even look up, let alone return your friendly hello. What I do know is those who tend to enjoy the portage the most are the ones who savor the scenery, don't carry too many burdens, and know when to get the hell out of the way.

24
Ingenious Nasty Beavers

"Canada was built on dead beavers."
MARGARET ATWOOD

Our initial plan was to camp at Whitefish campground. However, after being soured by the obnoxious campers down by the beach, Andy and I changed our minds. We had only seen a handful of paddlers since we started the Meanest Link in Huntsville 12 days prior and it was like shell shock to walk across the campground.

Unfortunately, there wasn't a legitimate interior campsite to stay on until we reached Tanamakoon Lake, a full 11-hour day of paddling and portaging for us. We went for it, paddling up the twisting Madawaska River, blocked by several beaver dams, mud-caked portages and a moose that refused to move out of our way when we tried to paddle past.

The name Madawaska comes from the Native Algonquian word Matouweskarini, meaning "people of the shallows." It's a fitting name for a labyrinth of weedy channels. Andy and I weren't ever lost on the Madawaska, but we were confused about our whereabouts several times. We were forced to backtrack and re-lift over several beaver dams, barriers of sticks and mud crafted by Algonquin's largest rodent. Further south, where the riverbanks are made of soil and not hard granite, beavers burrow into the soft shoreline. In the north, however, they're forced to build their own dens, basically a pile of sticks with a hollowed-out center. Water levels have to be maintained for the lodge to exist, which is why the beaver constructs dams. Beavers are intelligent creatures that get my respect — except when I'm clambering over their dams. Then they just become pesky rodents.

The beaver is an essential animal in Canadian history. Beaver pelts were central to the early Canadian trade economy. Some 200,000 pelts were exported each year during the height of the fur trade. And there are plenty of beavers now, especially along the Madawaska River.

But there was a time when the beaver was close to extinction: trapping and the fur trade between the 16th and 19th centuries that nearly exterminated the creature. During this period, felt hats made of the rodent's under-fur were all the rage in Europe. After the population of Russian and Baltic beavers was depleted, fur traders came looking for beavers in North America. It wasn't until the fickle fashion tastes changed to silk hats in the 1820s that the animals were saved from oblivion. Also, the realization that fumes from the nitrate of mercury used in the felt-making process affected the nerves of hatmakers and caused their speech to blur and nerves to twitch — hence the term "mad as a hatter" — also helped the public to lose interest.

Wildlife protection for animals, including the beaver, was one of the main rationales for creating Algonquin. Beaver numbers were still down when the park was formed, but just one year later Superintendent Peter Thomson reported that the beavers were "multiplying in numbers." By 1910, there were so many beavers roaming Algonquin they were perceived to be a nuisance. Orders went out for the rangers to begin trapping them. That ended in 1920 because market prices for the pelts weren't enough to warrant trapping anymore. More money was made by live-trapping the beavers and selling them off. The first year of this practise, 100 beavers were shipped to the United States for $30 each.

The mishmash of beaver dams and shallow channels that Andy and I had to navigate along the Madawaska became less problematic thanks to Andy's GPS, which allowed us to keep pointed in the right direction. I had also packed my SPOT, a satellite GPS messenger. Each night I'd push the "I'm Okay" button to let friends and family know our location and that we were still alive. My mother loved these updates. The device also features an emergency SOS button, which can trigger a rescue in an emergency.

The days are over when a paddler would head out into the woods, while friends and family hoped and prayed they'd come back alive. It took me a while to take to technology in the wilderness, but I've since adopted the old adage: If you stand in the way of progress you'll just get run over.

With all the affordable satellite communications options available today to outdoor adventurers and those who venture beyond the reach of cellular networks, we can now lessen our anxiety — and that of our loved ones — about getting lost, injured or worse. At the push of a button, a call for help can be transmitted to family or emergency responders along with GPS coordinates.

Packing a piece of technology to stay connected while you're trying to disconnect is a tough concept for some people. And while I would avoid traveling in the interior with others who insisted on listening to Lady Gaga on their iPod rather than the call of the loon, I don't believe the firepit should be the only hot spot out there. It's ludicrous to think that communications technology — which can be a lifeline should an emergency occur in the woods — represents some form of evil. I believe if there's a reliable and affordable way to stay connected to the civilized world, you'd be foolish not to make it a part of your safety gear.

25

Bob Dylan Went to Kids Camp

"I don't get homesick at camp; I get campsick at home."
ZACH DEAN (Camp Pathfinder Alumni)

It was dusk when we reached the western inlet of Tanamakoon Lake and jumped on the very first campsite, pitching our tent on a small island populated by a flock of Canada geese that had pooped everywhere. The geese weren't happy to share their island, and neither were we. But we tried our best to co-exist until morning.

The only good that came out of where we stayed was the invite that Andy and I received in the morning for a free breakfast from the neighboring Camp Tanamakoon. I'm a huge fan of youth camps (and of a free breakfasts!). I had worked as an outdoor educator in my 20s and easily recognized the traditional camp songs sung before and after breakfast.

Visiting Camp Tanamakoon refreshed the trip for me. It reminded me why places like Algonquin are so important. Imagine growing up and spending a summer canoe tripping in this wilderness — it would shape your life. Influential camp kids include Bob Dylan, Neil Diamond, Chevy Chase, Martha Stewart and Albert Einstein. Former Canadian Prime Minister Trudeau even went to Algonquin's Camp Ahmek. So did his son and Canada's current Prime Minister, Justin Trudeau.

Youth camps are one of the biggest treasures of Algonquin. The earliest youth group recorded paddling in the park was Bordentown Military Institute back in 1907. The first established camp, however, was an all-girls outfit named Camp Northway, established in 1908 on Cache Lake by Fannie Case. She was an educator from Rochester, New York. Miss Case was criticized heavily for bringing girls into the wilderness, as many believed canoe trips were too difficult for young women. She proved them wrong. The popularity of camp-organized canoe trips became the selling point of Camp Northway and other camps were quick to follow suit and adopted this activity in their marketing campaigns.

Camp Minnewawa on Lake of Two Rivers and Long Trail Camp on Little Joe Lake were both built in 1911. Renowned camp owner Taylor Statton (a.k.a. The Chief) brought Camp Ahmek to Algonquin's Little Wapomeo Island in 1921, and his wife Ethel opened up the girl's-only Camp Wapomeo in 1924.

Some camps — like Camp Arowhon, Camp Tamakwa and Camp Tanamakoon — became legendary, while others failed in their first year. Camp Pathfinder was established on Source Lake in 1914 by the Rochester educators Franklin Gray and William Bennett. It was Algonquin's second camp. Today it is the oldest camp still operating in Algonquin and is connected to the Meanest Link.

A visit to Camp Pathfinder had been in our plans. It's a tradition for Meanest Link paddlers to go off-route for the day and portage into Source Lake to say hello to the staff and kids. The camp helped create the Meanest Link and a selected group of boys have paddled the route every season for many years. Unfortunately, we had to forgo the tradition so Andy could make it to our take-out in time for him to return to work. It was no-brainer to choose to finish the trip with my canoe companion over making a quick visit to the camp.

Later that summer, I paddled back to Camp Pathfinder. I arrived on the day that an elite and limited group of campers was coming in after completing the Meanest Link. They were bruised and blistered, wearing tattered t-shirts and paddling aged cedar-canvas canoes. I could hear them long before spotting them, singing their camp's song while they paddled the last stretch of water of their difficult but rewarding journey.

Youth camps helped create most of the canoe routes in Algonquin. During Camp Pathfinder's early years, most trips were taken on nearby lakes, like Smoke and Ragged lakes. Camps were just too busy settling in on their island base camps to venture much further. However, by the mid-1920s, camps had broadened their tripping programs. In 1926, an exploratory route was forged down the Oxtongue and South River, and further to the Lake of Bays the following year. By the 1930s routes had expanded to the Nipissing River, Barron Canyon and down the Amable du Fond River to the Mattawa River and North Bay. Now, trips up in northern Quebec and James Bay have been added to some camp trip lists.

There's no question that camp life changes people for the better. To quote the current Camp Pathfinder director, Michael Sladden: "The values and experiences are timeless. Those lakes and forests are still the ultimate setting for fostering independence and positive life lessons."

I've done my fair share of taking kids into the park, from youth at-risk to college outdoor education students. And I know that it transforms them. A recent fall backpacking trip with a college group proved that.

It was my third-year backpacking in late fall along Algonquin's Western Uplands Trail with students in an college outdoor education program where I was an instructor. It was the third consecutive year of bad weather, and we had cold temperatures with a mixture of rain and snow. It was also the third year I had to take a group of students back to the parking lot two days into the seven-day trek.

Stephanie had complained about stomach pain shortly after we left the access point. The more we hiked, the worse it got. Ed also complained of a swollen ankle and wanted to leave the trip.

You don't mess around with severe stomach pain on a trip. So, the decision amongst the group was Stephanie needed to be evacuated, and Ed could be as well. The process was easy enough. There were two other trip leaders. They would continue on the trail with two-thirds of the students, and my group would take Stephanie and Ed back to the parking lot, then hike the loop counterclockwise. We hoped to meet up with the others in a couple of days.

By noon my group, plus Stephanie and Ed, were back in the parking lot. Another instructor came to pick up the injured students and take them to the closest hospital. Gear was re-sorted in packs and my remaining students returned to the trail, all feeling a bit unmotivated by the departure of the other two students. It made sense. The other two groups were well on their way into the hike and my group was starting all over again.

We reached the first lake just after dusk and used our headlamps to pitch the tents. Everyone seemed in a sullen mood, wondering if Stephanie and Ed were being examined at the hospital or sitting at home, on a comfortable couch drinking beer.

I used the satellite phone to check in. Ed's ankle had been wrapped and he had been sent home. Stephanie, however, was still in the hospital. The pain in her stomach was due to a ruptured cyst in her ovaries.

Taking her out was the right decision. But to be honest, I've become a bit jaded about taking students out backpacking in the off-season. It's all too common for students to pull the pin a day or two into a full week trip.

On a previous backpacking trip, I took five students back to the parking lot on day two while silently questioning how everyone could suddenly become mysteriously sick or injured. The year prior, a student had bailed on day three due to an ankle injury. The doctor note she provided me was fake, and I later found out it was her drug addiction that made her want to go home.

Drug addictions aside, I'm noticing a phobia some students have of spending a long period of time in the woods, especially when it's cold and wet. There's even a growing lack of passion for being out there. Even the students that complete a lengthy trip take a lot longer adjusting while they are out — or maybe it seems that way because I'm getting old and cranky.

On the trip where I had to take five students out on the second day, the entire group lacked skills and, more importantly, enthusiasm. When I asked them to hang their food packs they failed miserably with the straightforward task. Some food packs weren't hung — one was even used as a pillow. Even the ones that were hung were done poorly. A bear never visited us — thankfully. We were lucky.

I was angry at the students, but I know that negative energy is the worst way to get a point across. I chose to change tactics. I took one of the worst bear hangs — a pack that had been simply tied to the trunk of a small birch tree — and dragged it a few hundred meters back into the woods. When the students woke up and started searching, I turned my camera on and started filming. There was some panic when they couldn't find their food. When they discovered the bag, accusations of who was at fault began. It didn't inspire group unity — but heck, I enjoyed watching it all unfold.

After the packs were located, individual cooking groups made breakfast. All of them tried consuming the heaviest food items in their packs to reduce hiking loads. One group enjoyed bacon and hamburger patties pressed between water-soaked balls of Wonder Bread. Another group fried up 10 eggs. They had a dozen starting out, but two broke because they hung the carton on the side of someone's pack. I was amazed that only two eggs had become casualties.

The tension in the group peaked on day three of the seven-day trip. And believe me, in the wilderness, group conflict is far more problematic than nuisance bears and lightning strikes. Tension is a tossed salad of anxiety, anger, jealousy and revenge. At times my group seemed like *Lord of the Flies* played out in the interior of Algonquin. Groups separated, friends split, ethics were challenged.

I decided to let nature be the lead instructor during the trip. I was just going along for the ride. It worked. By day five, moods had brightened. We arrived at camp just prior to a hail storm, followed by a brief snowstorm. The temperature had dropped significantly, averaging four degrees Celsius. It was cold and wet. The students went about their business of setting up tents, tarp and gathering wood, happily oblivious to the weather. They had become used to the foul conditions, immersing themselves in their environment rather than battling against it. Around the evening campfire, there were stories of blinding snow squalls, exhausting uphill scrambles, and vomit due to dehydration. But there were also stories of scenic vistas, wildlife sightings and fun songs sung while on the trail. The group had acclimatized to life in the woods.

On the last evening, a potluck dinner was organized amongst all the remaining groups. The feast was an attempt to eat away any excess weight before the final hike out the next day. It was also a way for the students to merge back together.

I wandered around camp, listening to everyone share stories of their misadventure, as well as their enlightened comments about why they didn't want the trip to end.

It's interesting how time spent in nature can readjust our characters, allowing us to become familiar once again with wild places. These students left their modern comforts and roamed unprepared in a cold, wet and foreign environment. For the first few days, all of them questioned being there. They showed signs of anxiety and depression and wanted to go home. Seven days later, the remaining students walked out feeling confident, prepared, more connected to the wilderness and like better versions of themselves. More importantly, they all had a deep desire to come back. They proved that more time spent in the wilderness is one of the best ways to battle anxiety.

26
Is Algonquin Too Dangerous For Kids?

"They'll be ragged, dirty, and they'll stink when they get back; and they'll be as proud as they can be."

MICHAEL SLADDEN (camp director, Camp Pathfinder)

In June 1978, 12 boys and one leader from Saint John's School of Ontario drowned after their canoes capsized on Lake Timiskaming. It was a horrific tragedy. The only good that came of it were the drastic changes made to educate outdoor leaders on paddling safety. Canoe programs across Canada were re-examined and standards made. However, accidents still happen out there. So, the question is: should we stop taking kids out there?

In 2018, there was an event on Lake Simcoe with frightening parallels to the Timiskaming disaster. A high school group, heading out on their annual canoe trip, found themselves in trouble after a massive windstorm capsized the canoes of four of the 16 students and necessitated rescue by helicopter.

On a local news report, one of the lead teachers and the school's principal stated that they were unaware of the poor weather conditions approaching. Chat forums on Facebook and Twitter were littered with negative comments about their poor leadership. Weather networks had been warning of the upcoming storm all day.

Thankfully, all the students were wearing PFDs and had passed a swim test before embarking on the trip. Only four students were treated for mild hypothermia.

This event, and the drowning of a non-swimming student on a canoe trip in 2017 in Algonquin, has again stirred up the conversation about youth safety in the wilderness.

I wasn't there to witness the details that led to either accident. So, I have no right to judge anyone involved. I do, however, want people to be aware of the consequences of such accidents.

School administrators across North America are now canceling canoe tripping curriculums for students. Ontario's Durham School Board announced in 2018 that no outdoor club could continue their annual canoe trips. Penn State University's risk assessment determined activities such as hiking, running, backpacking and canoe tripping are too risky. The 169-member club, founded in 1920, isn't allowed to go outside anymore.

I've seen similar reactions where I teach part-time at college. My students now have to wear life jackets while doing a pond study or to gather water at the campsite. I understand it's better to be safe than sorry, but it seems to me things are getting a little out of hand. Overprotecting our youth has become a plague.

While administrators protect their careers from litigation, parents continue to bubble wrap their kids. Passionate, well trained, highly-certified, and well-seasoned instructors are getting fed up with it all. Many are retiring early or simply walking away and going back to teaching the basic boring classes in a confined classroom, rambling on like Charlie Brown's teacher while the kids play with their iPhones under their desks.

I too have started to question taking students out, but not because of my frustrations at over-coding rules and regulations. My desire to keep taking kids out in the woods overpowers this vexation. I'm more concerned about the students I'm taking out. In most of my 30-plus years of guiding youth out in the wilderness, I've done few evacuations. Recently, however, I did a dozen in one month, the majority of which were due to anxiety attacks.

Mental injury is the same as a physical injury. I'm not knocking the students who had such issues. I'm just concerned more rescues happen because of stress over being out in the wilderness instead of sprained ankles or cuts from a pocketknife.

So, what do we do about it? Do instructors gather in groups, get organized, try to stay passionate, attempt to calm the administrators and parents by making positive change?

More importantly, should leaders keep getting more certifications, gather sage advice from past instructors, get more bush time and gain more practical experience?

Or do we all just give up?

I remember a high school administrator I worked for who banned on-water activities completely. She thought I would give up on taking the groups of troubled kids out into the wild after that. But I don't give up that easily. I countered the absurd regulation by changing the proposed canoe trip into a backpacking trip. There were no rules against walking — not yet anyway.

Getting permission for this still wasn't easy. I had to jump through hoops to satisfy the paranoid administration, including filling out a 12-page document reminiscent of my taxes confirming my trip leading experience. One chief concern was whether I could handle a bear encounter.

Despite detailing the unlikeliness of encountering a bear — and my successful handling such rare encounters — the trip almost didn't go ahead. The administration's handwringing and misplaced fear left me frustrated.

Cutbacks, rising costs and the ever-looming threat of litigation are all reasons why school boards are more hesitant than ever to green light wilderness trips.

It's the students who miss out. It's well documented outdoor programs encourage mental and physical health. Outdoor adventure experiences increase self-confidence, as students are encouraged to navigate new challenges, manage risks and practice self-care. Immersed in nature, kids can't help but engage with the curriculum. Plus, they skip fewer classes — there's 100-percent attendance for classes in the wilderness.

We had discussed what the students should do if they encountered an unwelcome ursine, but there were no bear encounters during our weeklong trek in the woods. The only wildlife sighting of note was a porcupine. It was living under an old outhouse and caused one student to let out an unholy scream in the middle of the night. Oh, and a family of raccoons that tried to steal a pair of smelly sneakers.

I found out on our return that it was the high school itself that saw all the action. While we were playing it safe in the wilderness, a black bear took a stroll through the schoolyard on its way to feast at one of the town's fast food restaurant dumpsters. The high school principal ordered a lockdown, and a tactical police unit arrived to gun down the bear. The incident made national news.

The principal didn't see the irony of the situation.

Risk isn't often as obvious as a 400-pound black bear with a Whopper craving, but it's a part of everyday life. Risk exists in the wilderness and on the playground. It's on the road, on the water and even in your home. It's inescapable. It's better to learn to manage risk and grow from that valuable experience, rather than try to hide from it.

27

Civilization on the Horizon

"Cottage is the palace of humble man!"
MEHMET MURAT ILDAN

After having seconds of bacon and eggs, Andy and I left the comforts of Camp Tanamakoon and continued on the final leg of our trip. Our plan for the day was portaging to Smoke Lake, which would finish our upstream paddle on the Madawaska River, and then heading downstream on our last river of the trip, the Oxtongue.

The portage leading into Smoke Lake was a tough one, up and over a mound of granite carpeted with mixed deciduous forest. At least the wind wasn't howling across Smoke Lake, as it usually is.

Smoke is one of the few lakes with land leases. Algonquin has over 300 cottages on several lakes; Smoke, Canoe, Cache and Rock hold the majority. In the early 1900s, cottages were used to promote tourism and gather taxes for the government. The first two lots were made available on Canoe Lake in 1905. The leasing program was at its peak in 1920 when the Ontario government became desperate for money. However, by 1954 the government had changed its tune. They wanted the cottages to go, feeling they took away the wildness of Algonquin and occupants were given a 21-year lease. The lease has been extended three times since, most recently in October 2016, enabling cottagers to occupy their cottage lots up to December 31, 2038.

The cottages are a source of debate. Some believe cottages don't belong in a wilderness setting; others argue that they are an integral part of the park and have been for more than 100 years.

The Canadian Parks and Wilderness Society (CPAWS) opposed the last extension of the lease, stating "the park has to be managed for ecological integrity." Norm Richards, managing director of Ontario Parks from 1981 to 1999, views the cottages as part of the park's heritage. John Winters, Algonquin's park superintendent from 1996 to 2011, describes the leaseholders as "park lovers first and cottage leaseholders second."

For comparison's sake, the cottages take up 0.02 percent of the park, while Algonquin's campgrounds receive more than 100,000 campers annually. Day-use visitors reach almost 200,000 annually and interior use is close to 300,000 campers every year. There are also restrictions when leasing a cottage in Algonquin. It can't be used as a permanent residence, and leasers can't expand, sublet or alter shorelines.

The owners pay lease and service fees to the province along with property taxes. And the taxes went up — way up — bringing thousands of dollars to the coffers of Ontario Provincial Parks.

28

Down the Oxtongue

"My favorite places on earth are the wild waterways where the forest opens its arms and a silver curve of river folds the traveler into its embrace."

RORY MacLEAN

The last watershed on our trip was the Oxtongue. Andy and I had two ways to reach it. The first was to head north and portage from Smoke Lake across Highway 60 to Canoe Lake, and head west through Bonita Lake and Tea Lake. Tea Lake dam is where the Oxtongue River begins. The second option was to simply paddle Smoke Creek, connecting Smoke Lake and Tea Lake and avoiding the portage. We took the shortcut but in retrospect, we shouldn't have by-passed classic Canoe Lake. Too many important events have happened on this lake, including the birth of Mowat Lodge and the death of painter Tom Thomson.

Mowat Lodge originated after Shannon Fraser and wife, Annie, took over a boarding house from what remained of the Gilmour and Company mill in 1903. It opened as a lodge in 1913, burned down once in 1920, and again 1931. Renowned artist Tom Thomson first stayed at the lodge in 1912. He did it first to get out of the rain, and he continued his visits until his mysterious death in 1917. His bloated corpse, complete with a bloody ear and copper fishing wire wrapped around his ankle was found a week after his canoe was seen floating empty on Canoe Lake. Was it death by mishap (Thomson liked his whisky), or was it murder? Rumor grew of an affair with a woman living on Canoe Lake. Other's gossiped about a suicide or foul play due to an unpaid debt, or a difference of opinion about the war effort.

Regardless of how he died, Thomson managed to give life to one of the most famous batches of Canadian painters, the Group of Seven. He invited each and every member to Algonquin to paddle and paint in the interior of the park. In return, they created an art form that truly depicted what Canada was all about: the rocks, the trees, and the rugged wilderness. No painter had done that before.

Group of Seven member J.E.H. Macdonald led a number of artists and Tom Thomson disciples to a rocky outcrop on Canoe Lake, and placed a cairn there. A plaque on it reads:

"He lived humbly but passionately with the wild. It made him brother to all untamed things of nature. It drew him apart and revealed itself wonderfully to him. It sent him out from the woods only to show these revelations through his art. And it took him to itself at last."

The inscription makes no mention of how Thomson died; it simply invokes his dedication to sharing the beauty of what he experienced in Algonquin.

I'm familiar with the Oxtongue. I've paddled the river many times in the past. It's a leisurely float through a very accessible but uncrowded wild area, especially after it leaves Algonquin's western border. Of course, this wasn't the case when Andy and I started paddling it. The dam was closed for construction on the nearby highway and only a mere trickle of water was flushing down.

As a result, we found ourselves walking the canoe down each shallow rapid. Making it worse was the smell. The river reeked of rotten vegetation. A major spring flood had also left some snags blocking the way. I kept thinking of the movie Groundhog Day. Andy and I had gone back in time and found ourselves, once again, wading a rocky river bed. At least it was the last couple of days of our trip rather than the first, and we were going downstream instead of up. I still have nightmares of my time spent walking up the Big East River in the first week of our trip.

The Oxtongue watershed teems in history. Native groups and even missionaries and fur traders paddled and portaged, entering the Algonquin Dome by way of the Oxtongue. So did the majority of engineers and explorers searching for the place to build the War of 1812 canal. Surveyor James Dickson paddled up the Oxtongue and wrote about the country that is now Algonquin in his book, *Camping in the Muskoka Region* (1886).

"Come with me and we will spend a summer holiday in this sylvan retreat, where, though we can reach it in a few hours' travel, we will be completely cut off from the busy haunts of men."

Dickson's description of his wilderness journal helped spawn a letter to the government by another land surveyor, Alexander Kirkwood, to create a park in the region explored by James Dickson.

Peter Thomson, the first chief ranger of Algonquin, also entered the park by way of the Oxtongue in 1893. He was traveling to Canoe Lake to build the first park headquarters.

Painter Tom Thomson's first canoe and painting trip in Algonquin was on the Oxtongue. He must have loved it because he later invited a number of the Group of Seven to join him there. A.Y. Jackson camped at Tea Lake dam with him to paint in 1914, where he created one of his most memorable paintings, *The Red Maple*. Thomson also convinced Lawren Harris to paint the spring season on the Oxtongue River in 1924. That painting made Harris' career. A.J. Casson also followed Thomson's advice on the Oxtongue, as well as Frederick Varley and Arthur Lismer. Trust me, if you paddle the river, you'll know why they were inspired there. It's a tranquil spot, except when there's no water.

The Oxtongue was a busy place at one time. It was a main waterway trail entering the park. Today, you would be hard-pressed to spot another paddler traveling the river, especially the lower half that exits the park's southwest corner and forms a separate waterway park. People don't seem to paddle it. Maybe because it's close to Highway 60 and traffic can be heard faintly along some sections, or maybe paddlers assume Algonquin Provincial Park has more to offer.

We spent our day on it was mostly floating on a gentle current, listening to the brook trout slurp bugs from the water's surface and counting the number of turtles sunbathing on half-submerged logs. Often, I'd simply gawk at all the damselflies and dragonflies flitting along the river's edge. Algonquin contains just under 100 recorded dragonfly species, the majority of which can be found along the Oxtongue River. Chalk-fronted corporal dragonflies and Hagen's bluet damselflies inhabit the calm bays of the river. The translucent, sapphire blue insects hovered around my head as I paddled, snacking on bothersome mosquitoes and deer flies. I spotted the provincially rare zebra clubtail soaring over clear, sandy-bottom sections of the river. But the most notable of all the flying insects were the ebony jewel-wing, with its striking iridescent green body, and the river jewel-wing, the tips of its wings appearing to have been dipped in ink. Both species had the agreeable habit of perching on the bow of the canoe or the blade of my paddle, or even on me.

The Oxtongue has a number of shallow swifts and a few significant rapids and cascades: Whiskey Rapids, Split Rock Rapids, Twin Falls, Gravel Falls and Ragged Falls. But for the most part, the water meanders along. Calm stretches of river wind around pine-clad bluffs on one side and spill quietly past islands covered in alder and dogwood on the other. Much of the scenery remains similar to what surveyor Alexander Sheriff described in his 1829 journal: "a level, sandy valley, timbered chiefly with balsam, tamarack, and poplar, beyond which, however, the hardwood rising grounds are seldom a mile distant on either side."

Just beyond Twin Falls, the Oxtongue leaves Algonquin's western border and becomes its own park. Andy and I left Algonquin and had our last "wild" camp alongside the 10-meter high Gravel Falls. This is a smaller cascade just upstream of the much larger 30-meter Ragged Falls, which typically swarms with dozens of tourists gawking at what's rated as one of the best waterfalls in the province.

By mid-morning the next day we had portaged around Ragged Falls, an amazing drop in elevation, and dropped by the Algonquin Outfitters' store on Oxtongue Lake. There to greet us was Gord Baker, one of the original masterminds behind the Meanest Link.

Gord spent time with us and reminisced about past Meanest Link paddlers.

He had some favorites, like Will Lougheed and Chris Bosworth, who had set out in June of 2008, planning to finish in 15 days. They did it in only nine. The trip was in dedication to a friend who passed away the day before they embarked (Clarke Wallace). C.W 1 was ornamented on their canoe. In 2010, Matt Strickland and Madeleine Woods completed their trip in an astonishing seven-and-a-half days. They currently hold the record for the speediest journey.

Another favorite of Gord Baker's Meanest Linkers are Jeff Burdzy and Luke van Koeverden. They completed the route in 12 days, in early May. High water created a huge challenge for them, as did the blackflies, high winds, constant rain and even snow. Baker gives them extra credit because, as alumni of Camp Pathfinder, they chose to do the route Pathfinder-style, which means they paddled it using a classic red cedar-canvas canoe from the Camp Pathfinder fleet. They also carried all their food with them. They used no food drops. Gord placed their trip in the epic category.

29

You Shall Not Pass!

Sign, sign, everywhere a sign
Blockin' out the scenery
Breakin' my mind
Do this, don't do that
Can't you read the sign?

THE FIVE MAN ELECTRICAL BAND

On our fifteenth day, it was time for Andy and me to cheat again. The water issues on the Oxtongue River grew worse, and the section below Oxtongue Lake looked as if some giant had dropped a big bag of marbles across the riverbed. Only a pathetic amount of water squeezed through an almost dried up boulder garden and we resorted to accepting a lift around the central rapids from Rich Swift of Algonquin Outfitters. It saved us a good two kilometers of portaging and walking the river.

Beyond the last major rapid, the Oxtongue seemed to deepen a bit, at least enough for us to finally float the canoe. It was a beautiful stretch, the last bit of wilderness on the trip. Everything was sublime, except for a minor private land issue. The old portage around the last cascade in the river is on private property. No Trespassing signs littered the place and the landowner immediately came out to inform us we were on her property and she wouldn't allow us to pass.

I found it odd that a paddler couldn't portage around a major falls on a major river. I thought free passage was a Canadian law, but the landowner informed me that I was wrong. Rather than get annoyed with her, I calmly told her we were on the second last day of a multi-week canoe trip around Algonquin Park and this was the second last portage of the 93 we had to do before completing our epic journey. I'm not sure whether the landowner felt sorry for us or just couldn't be bothered listening to me grovel anymore, but she decided to let us through, firmly stating that it would only be just this once. Andy gave out a giggle and said that wouldn't be a problem — we'd never do this crazy route again!

I made mention of the land dispute on national radio when I returned from my trip. Two years later a deal was made. Today a portage, marked by a government portage sign, exists alongside the waterfall.

One minute we were being scolded by a landowner, and the next we were invited to camp in another's backyard. Jack and Peggy Hurly offered us a portion of their lawn to pitch our tent on, and their yard hose to fetch water. It was an absolute Shangri-La. Andy and I had no idea where we were going to camp our last night out. We were now deep into the depth of cottage country, and there was no legitimate place to put a tent. Now, we not only had a cozy place to stay, but also a fascinating host. Jack happens to be a legendary canoe builder, and it was an honor to have the grand tour of his workshop and to listen to his stories of time spent in Algonquin, building the famed cedar-canvas Pathfinder canoes. Andy and I repaid the Hurley's kindness by staying late the next morning to help Jack canvas a canoe. What a privilege!

Jack's workshop is an oddity, a mix between a hoarder's barn and a canoe chronologist's shrine. There was the regular smell of varnish in the air and cedar shavings covering the floor. Wood for ribs was stored in the rafters, rolls of canvas were bundled up in the corners, and skeletons of canoes in various stages of repair were scattered throughout. Most notable, however, was what adorned all four walls — a collage of old photographs, some depicting celebrity canoeists and historic scenes of Algonquin throughout time. Others were just random pictures of people, places and things that meant little to the world of canoeing and Algonquin. It was surreal.

When asked about the pictures he's plastered on his walls each and every day since he can remember, which some visitors may perceive to be over-the-top chaos, Jack explained that they were his way of surrounding himself with history. He's a traditionalist who has always carefully tripped through Algonquin paddling in a wood-canvas canoe and portaging with a rugged canvas pack and wannigan with a leather tumpline. He believes that traditional materials have a stronger spirit than modern-day fabrics. The vibrant colors of the wood, the aesthetics of a caned seat and the smell of wood smoke permeating a canvas pack, are all qualities drawn from the natural environment.

Before leaving the Hurleys, Jack left us with his view of the park.

"I took my eulogy about seven years ago, and one of the questions was...Where and when were you happiest? His answer "All of my happiness has been in Algonquin Park; it's the most beautiful place in the world, don't ya think?"

The last day of our trip was a quick one. We only had two large cottage lakes to paddle across, and we even cheated on the last portage. It was a two-kilometer road, called Portage Road, and we simply hitched a ride to cross it. It was one of the funniest moments of our trip to be quite honest.

The main reason we cheated a bit throughout the trip was that Andy had a scant 16 days of holidays. I thought it would take 20 days for us to complete the trip. Andy had initially planned to leave the trip on day 16 and let me continue alone. However, by day 12, he had changed his tune. He wanted to cross the finish line. Finishing together was a far better way to complete the Link, I thought. A change of plans was in order.

We had to make a few shortcuts. First was the boat shuttle across Algonquin's biggest lake, Opeongo; otherwise, it's more than half a day's paddle. Unfortunately, we skipped the side route to visit Camp Pathfinder. And then there was hitching the ride along the lower Oxtongue rapids and the two kilometers of Portage Road.

Not long after completing the trip, we learned about the controversy.

I had mentioned our shortcutting the traditional route in my CBC Radio interviews and posted our shortcuts online throughout the trip, along with photos and text. After writing about our change in plans, we were the targets of an online lashing. A few Meanest Link alumni disagreed with our shortcuts and labeled us cheaters. Some even claimed we didn't deserve to travel the route and had disgraced the institution of Meanest Link paddlers. Ouch!

On one hand, all the others who had completed the route kept to the customary ways. But the cheater label is a hard one to stick when you're honest about what's going on. Should I have kept to the plan and left my canoe mate behind, just so I could follow the rules? Or were we right to alter our trip so we could cross the finish line together?

In typical 21st-century fashion, I let the device that had initiated the debate decide our fate. I posted the question to Facebook and Twitter. Five respondents cursed us, but thousands agreed with our decision. Andy and I would complete the Meanest Link together, guilt-free.

My online posts and CBC Radio interviews also earned Andy and I a bit of a fan base. It's not as if we had groupies, but a fair number of cottagers lounging on their docks asked us if we were the crazy guys paddling around Algonquin. We even came across a sign nailed to a tree that read: "Kevin and Andy, Trails and Tamaracks welcomes you to the Lake of Bays."

The Tamarack posting was amusing, but our last hour of paddling towards Huntsville was hilarious. We had unwittingly chosen the day of the big Huntsville bathtub race to finish. Helicopters buzzed overhead, speedboats and Jet-Skis churned up the water around us. A police boat even pulled us over for a ride check. In the confusion, Andy and I found ourselves in the center of the bathtub race, and the organizer belittled us through the loudspeaker for getting in everyone's way.

Hundreds of people lined the Huntsville docks, but only a handful were there to witness Andy and I complete our epic trip. Gord Baker from Algonquin Outfitters and a couple of his staff helped us unload and portage through the fans of the bathtub race. For us, the ending was perfect. Rather than having banners hung and people cheering for us at the finish line, our accomplishments were overshadowed by a bunch of locals propelling themselves across the water with motorized bathtubs. How ironic!

You might think that, after 16 days, we'd be craving the company of other people, or at least a chance to drink a beer and feast on a greasy burger and fries. However, the return was an absolute culture shock. Both Andy and I already missed the wilderness and had a tough time adjusting.

That was the proof I was looking for — that feeling of association with the natural world one feels after spending a long period of time within it. It was verification that the desire to immerse oneself in a wilderness setting can overpower the addiction to civilized comforts. That's what happened to Andy and me.

To quote John Muir:

> *"Thousands of tired, nerve-shaken, over-civilized people are beginning to find out going to the mountains is going home; that wilderness is a necessity..."*

Epilogue

Andy ruined his left knee on this trip, his wife rolls her eyes every time I mention the Meanest Link, and he doesn't talk much about our time out there. I think I got more from paddling and portaging around Algonquin than he did.

My life was in turmoil at the time. My wife was about to leave me; I saw how drastically attitudes were changing with the youth I was guiding in the woods and I wanted to quit the job I'd done for over 30 years; more drownings had occurred and school administrators were running scared; my outdoor education colleagues were terrified of the future of education, conservation and outdoor ethics; and many of my friends were rating Algonquin as an overcrowded zoo. It was like walking out of the theatre where you watched the most bizarre but inspirational movie of all time.

I created a film of our trip and went on tour across North America for a year. Over 15,000 people listened to my story. They laughed at our mishaps and setbacks during endless portages, stolen whisky, and billions of mosquitoes. It was an enjoyable experience, but I also started each presentation by clearly stating I would never do the Meanest Link again.

Six years later, I yearn for it.

Life has improved. I grew less dumbfounded by the separation, less dependent on anti-depressants, slept better through the night, became more positive about our youth protecting wilderness. And when my daughter insisted that I start dating, I found love again.

What I crave is to be out there on the Meanest Link again, portages be damned. Visiting Algonquin throughout my life has formed the person I am today. My parents took me to the park as an infant. That piece of woods and water has molded me, calmed me, and given me direction in my life.

Yes, I'd definitely paddle around Algonquin again. Forget the countless portages, nasty mosquitoes, unethical campers, obscene amount of logging roads, disappearing wildlife, stolen whisky and crazed marathon-style elitists. This piece of wilderness amongst ever-encroaching development is my saving grace. It always will be.

TIPS BEFORE YOU GO

Do We Have Enough Whisky?

*"Too much of anything is bad,
but too much good whiskey is barely enough."*
MARK TWAIN

Packing for an extended trip can be a mixed bag of anticipatory excitement blended with substantial anxiety. While packing for the Meanest Link, I lived between to the two and my home became cluttered with camp gear, dried food, stove fuel and flasks of whisky.

To deal with the 93 portages on the Meanest Link, Andy and I had to single-carry our gear. On past trips, we usually do double carries on portages — first the canoe and the food barrel, then the two remaining gear packs. This time was different. We needed to pack like backpackers. Nothing too extreme — we didn't cut the ends off our toothbrushes to save a quarter of a gram. But we did leave behind enough luxuries to allow Andy to shoulder a medium-size pack and the canoe, and me the rest of our gear in one massive canoe pack.

PACKING TIPS

To reduce what gets packed, I set out my "must-have" items and figure out a way to reduce them. Some standards items, like a camp saw or ax, aren't essential on every trip. Second, I look at how to use items for multiple functions. And third, I review my luxury items — pillow, camp chair, extra underwear — and make a firm decision about whether they're worth the weight.

The major bulk inside a camp pack usually comes from three essential items: a tent, sleeping bag and clothes. I always opt for the smallest and lightest tent I can find. To me, my tent is a dog house — nothing more than a place to sleep. A tarp becomes the center of my campsite during foul weather.

For a sleeping bag, I opt for down fill rather than synthetic. Down is lighter and compacts smaller than a football, while a synthetic bag is bulkier. The only disadvantage of a down bag is that it's useless if it gets wet, while a sodden synthetic bag will at least offer some warmth.

I often find that clothing boggs trippers down. If our trip had been earlier in the year, I'd have packed long johns, a toque and a layer of wool and fleece. But Andy and I headed out on the Meanest Link in early summer. An extra pair of quick-dry pants, shirt, lightweight fleece or sweater, rain jacket a couple of pairs of high-tech synthetic underwear and a few pairs of socks were all I needed. I planned to do laundry on a warm, sunny day halfway through the trip.

Compression bags are the secret ingredient to making a pack smaller. Sleeping bag, clothes, tarp and tent are all stuffed away, squeezed in to their smallest possible sizes. I even place my tent fly and tent body in two separate bags. The fly will always be wet in the morning, from evening rain or morning dew. Packing it on its own helps keep the tent body drier, and therefore lighter.

FOOD

Food was the biggest issue for us on the Meanest Link. I had calculated we would need 20 days, later shortened to 16, to complete the trip. To carry rations for that length of time and maintain our dreams of a single-carrying all the portages would have forced us to eat gruel the entire trip. That wasn't an option.

At home, I dehydrated cheap, lightweight, delicious and nutritious meals and organized them in four parcels. One went with us for the first five days; the other three were sent out to pick-up locations along the way — the Rain Lake access, the town of Brent, and Opeongo Outfitters. Each parcel also contained stove fuel, toilet paper and a fresh whisky supply.

The whisky choice for the trip was Black Grouse. It was just a blended Scotch, not a luxurious single malt. But it was free. I was lucky enough to know a sales rep for Beam, a large whisky company, who wished me luck and handed me a box of 50 ml mini liquor bottles. It took me more than an hour to pour the 40 tiny bottles into four larger containers, each color-coded to its corresponding drop-off.

I spent a good month dehydrating enough food and making up recipes to last the full length of the trip. Drying homemade food is by far the most economical way to prepare long-lasting camp meals. Removing the moisture reduces between 80 to 90 percent of the food's weight, lightening your food pack considerably.

It's not that those store-bought dehydrated meals aren't palatable or wholesome, even though some of those meals give me a bad case of the toots. Backcountry gourmands have come a long way from eating breakfasts of green-powdered eggs and dinners of mock shepherd's pie more akin to savorless cardboard. However, with pre-packaged meals starting at roughly $14 each, dehydrating your own food can save a lot of money.

I picked up a good dehydrator for less than $100. I also used my kitchen oven, placing food items on the oven racks, using a cookie sheet for sauces and baking on the lowest temperature possible. It took six to eight hours for similar results to those of my commercial dehydrator, which can dehydrate in half the time.

Sauces are great for dehydrating. One jar of spaghetti sauce placed in the dehydrator or oven is reduced to a thin slice of what looks like fruit leather. Once in camp, simply place a small amount of the dried sauce in a ½ cup of boiling water, and it will magically transform into the original spaghetti sauce.

Vegetables are also easy to dehydrate. I routinely spend the winter months buying up different veggies that are on sale and drying them in bulk. Some of my favorites are broccoli, celery, green and red peppers, mushrooms, zucchini, corn, peas, and eggplant.

Meat takes a lot more preparation, because it must be cooked before it can be dried. Some meats, such as ground beef, should also be rinsed repeatedly with hot water to eliminate grease and reduce the chances of bacteria forming. I prefer drying ground turkey or ground venison, which contain less fat and are therefore less likely to spoil on a trip.

I also prefer to buy certain dried foods at bulk-food stores. Onions really stink up the house when dried in the dehydrator, and I can't seem to get banana chips or pineapple slices to look as appetizing as the ones I can get at the store.

The food and whisky were stored in a small 30-liter barrel, placed at the bottom of Andy's pack.

The canoe barrel's story goes back to the mid-1980s when a group of canoe guides from Ottawa, including Wally Schaber, one of Bill Mason's canoe buddies, experimented with packing their food and gear in olive barrels picked up at delicatessens and yard sales. The intention was to see if the watertight containers would keep their contents dry while paddling extreme northern rivers in Quebec. They did and now you can pick up 30- and 60-liter barrels at most outdoor stores.

The plastic olive barrel is the modern, waterproof version of a wannigan. However, just like using the traditional wannigan, it's a love-and-hate relationship. The barrel has all the advantages of the conventional wooden box — the lid can even double as a cutting board — but in no way is the thing comfortable to carry. At least it doesn't rely exclusively on a tumpline system. I strongly recommend paying the extra cost for a high-quality barrel harness. You'll thank me when you hit the portage.

Some canoeists opt to use barrels for keeping their food safe from critters. They're a great system to keep everything dry and odor-free and they can come in handy when traveling in the far north where there are no tall trees to hang your food. They will keep out squirrels and mice. But in no way should a canoe barrel be confused with a bear barrel. In the last few years, there have been numerous reports of campers who placed a food barrel right beside their tent and woke up to the sounds of a bear smashing it to pieces. If a bear can break into an automobile with one swing of a paw, then a thin plastic barrel is no match for it.

TENT

Our tent was a two-person design. It was a new purchase for the trip, and I made sure to choose a model that would be lightweight but comfortable for two grown men. The tent had lots of little extras, such as side pockets and a ceiling hammock for gear storage, center hook to dangle a flashlight from, color-coded clips and poles for easier set up, secondary guy lines for tightening the tent down in harsh conditions, and a light color fabric that allows in more light and brightens up your morning on grey days.

You don't have to spend a fortune on a tent to get a good one. Just look for a design that has good ventilation. A separate fly over the tent body is important. The more mesh the main structure has, the better. The more ventilation, the more control over heat and moisture. Double doors also vent better than one. Keep the doors perpendicular to the prevailing winds. Door zippers are the first place to gain moisture and let the wind and rain in.

I've owned several tents with various shapes and sizes, from the spacious cabin style to the classic A-frame. I prefer the geodesic dome, however. Its crossing pole structure makes it free standing and quite stable in a wind storm. It also gives you the best space to weight ratio.

When it comes to tent storage, there are the rollers, and then there are the crammers. The rollers painstakingly lay out the tent, fold it in thirds, place the poles at one end, and then roll everything up in a cigar shape. I'm a crammer and merely open up the storage bag and start stuffing everything in. I use two separate compression sacks, one for the main tent and another for the fly, because the tent fly is always wetter than the tent body.

CAMP STOVE

Some people collect stamps or GI Joe dolls. I collect camp stoves. I own stoves that run on butane, propane, alcohol and white gas. I also own half-a-dozen stick stoves. So, choosing which one to bring along was left for Andy to decide. He went with an MSR Simmer Lite white gas stove. It was a good choice. It was light and efficient. We just had to decide how much fuel we needed to store at each food drop.

The amount of fuel needed on a trip has so many variables, including fuel type, the air temperature, wind and design of a windscreen used, the stove's maximum heat output (measured in BTU), and even the type of pots and pans used. Overall, however, the best way to judge your fuel consumption is to plan 40 minutes of cooking time for dinner and 20 minutes for preparing a hot breakfast. Andy and I planned a food drop every five days. That added up to four dinners — two hours and 40 minutes of burning time — and four breakfasts — one hour and 10 minutes. Then we added an extra hour for a couple of hot soups for lunch on cold and rainy days. So, that's a little more than five hours of fuel for each five-day segment. The MSR burns quick and hot, and with a pump/fuel bottle it will use up a one-liter bottle of fuel every three days, which means we planned for two liters for five days, just to be on the safe side.

The last thing we did while packing was to be religious about measuring out proper portions of things like sunscreen, bug repellent, and toilet paper, most of which we ended up being too fanatical about. The mosquitoes were so bad we had to purchase more bug repellent when we got to the Brent Store on Cedar Lake; and I got the trots on day seven and had to use moss before our next toilet paper resupply. I should have remembered what Roald Amundsen when he once said, *"Adventure is just bad planning."*

CANOE CHOICE

Andy and I settled on using my 16-foot Nova Craft Prospector canoe. It's made of aramid, a generic version of Kevlar, and weighs just under 40 pounds. By infusing aramid cloth with high-impact resistant vinylester resin, Nova Craft has created a canoe with an incredible strength-to-weight ratio — perfect for paddling around Algonquin.

But why a Prospector model?

I found my very first canoe at the dump. It was a Prospector design, made of fiberglass, had three keels, and bore no company logo — just a roadrunner sticker affixed to the bow. I brought it home and patched it up. I used it do do my research for my first two paddling guidebooks. I called her *Gertrude,* named for Katherine Hepburn's canoe in the classic '80s film, *On Golden Pond.*

I eventually expanded my canoe collection and bought a second-hand boat — again a Prospector, made of fiberglass. I paddled it solo down the full length of the Missinaibi River. I was in my mid-twenties and knew little about running whitewater, but I had watched Bill Mason's National Film Board films over and over again. He too liked to paddle a Prospector.

The Prospector is not perfect at anything, but it's pretty good at everything. If I could only own one canoe, it would make good sense to choose a Prospector. The shape is symmetrical, meaning both bow and stern are the same shape. This allows you to paddle tandem, as well as solo. You merely sit in the front seat, trim the boat by shifting ballast and then paddle stern first. Asymmetrical hulls don't allow for that option.

Depending on its length, the Prospector is suited for a short day-trip as well as extended time exploring the wilderness. The design is typically deep and wide, with a substantial arch in the bottom. They're designed to carry heavy loads and manage waves on lakes and in rapids. The design has lots of rocker for maneuverability, and when heeled over while soloing, both ends rise nicely out of the water.

The Prospector was first manufactured by Chestnut Canoe Company of Fredericton, New Brunswick. That company no longer exists, but more than a dozen manufacturers are still making the design, some mimicking the original more closely than others. My favorite over the years has been the 16-foot Nova Craft Prospector, made in London, Ontario, Canada.

Shamefully, my loyalty swayed a couple times. I purchased a Cronjie design and a Bob Special. They're beautiful boats, but they don't get wet as much as my Prospector.

WATER TREATMENT

Our water filter stopped working while we took a break on the Nipissing where Loontail Creek flows in from the southeast. It's unfortunate when that particular piece of gear breaks down on a trip. The days are gone when a paddler could dip their cup over the gunwale of the canoe and drink straight from lake or river. Honestly, I'm not entirely sure it was ever wise to do so.

In any case, there's no way I will drink unfiltered water. I have had beaver fever twice in my life and it's not pleasant. The culprit, Giardia lamblia, is a tiny cyst that can get into the water cycle by being deposited in the feces of an infected animal. The typical host is a beaver, which is how this water-born pathogen got its nickname. But it can be deposited by any mammal, including humans.

Ten Giardia cysts are all it takes to infect your body. The microscopic protozoan, measuring 21 microns in length (the tip of a sewing needle measures 700 microns), hatches inside the small intestine with an incubation period from five days to several months. It reproduces like wildfire, establishes a colony, and then has a little party in your gut, making you feel as if Montezuma has moved north to seek his revenge.

Symptoms can be severe or completely unnoticeable. The noticeable ones include diarrhea, abdominal cramps, fatigue, weight loss, flatulence, and nausea — not a pleasant experience while being away from flush toilets and a local pharmacy. With shorter trips so common these days, most trippers don't develop symptoms until they've returned home. Left untreated giardia can cause severe problems. Both times I was afflicted antibiotic treatment took more than a month.

There are occasionally a few other nasties floating around in the water supply. E. coli can give a nasty case of the trots. Klebsiella pneumoniae causes pneumonia, and Salmonella can give you a bad case of food poisoning or a bout of typhoid fever. Plus, don't forget about the surface pollutants like gas fuel, pesticides and heavy metals from old mine sites. All of these dangers are good reasons to treat water where ever you are canoeing.

Boiling is the most common method to kill germs. A rolling boil for five minutes will eliminate most of everything, but just having the water come to a rolling boil is sufficient enough to get rid of most protozoa, bacteria and even viruses. The problem with boiling water is it's quite simply a waste of stove fuel. It also takes up too much time and canoeists end up not drinking enough throughout the day.

Chemical treatment or a UV system are two other options for cleaning water. Both work well in killing most of the nasties out there. My choice, however, is a water filter. The pump ones are handy, and I can pump and drink. Even better is a gravity filter, which luckily, I brought as a backup system.

With gravity-fed systems, you fill one plastic bag up with lake water and hang it up higher than the empty bag. The water is filtered through a hose and a filter cartridge. The system makes water collection so quick and easy that there's less chance of becoming dehydrated.

Water filters work by straining out pathogens. The purity of the water filtered relies on the size of the filter's pores. Any pore size of two microns or smaller will get rid of protozoa, like giardia, and most bacteria. However, a pore size of less than 0.4 microns is needed to remove viruses, like Hepatitis A and Norovirus, and some very small bacteria. Fortunately, there's no need to be concerned about viruses in an environment like Algonquin. Water-soluble pollutants, like heavy metals associated with mining, also can't be removed by the average camper's filter.

Thankfully, Andy and I packed a spare water filter. We just filled our water containers and moved on down the river.

Check out the story on YouTube

I filmed the entire story of Andy and I paddling around Algonquin. The video series (same title as the book) is available on my YouTube channel KCHappyCamper.

About the Author

Kevin Callan (aka The Happy Camper) is the author of 17 books, including the best-selling *The Happy Camper* and his incredibly popular series of paddling guides. He's a notable public speaker and frequent guest on radio and television. Kevin is also a regular contributor, blogger and columnist for *Explore* and *Paddling Magazine* and has won several National Magazine Awards. *Canadian Geographic* has labelled him one of the nation's top modern-day trailblazers.

PRAISE FOR

Once Around Algonquin — an Epic Canoe Journey

"Get ready for the canoe trip of a lifetime! Kevin Callan has written an instant classic in *Once Around Algonquin*, the story of Kevin and his pal Andy celebrating their 50th birthdays by taking on the legendary 'Meanest Link,' the toughest, longest, craziest — and most satisfying paddle and portage ever imagined."
ROY MacGREGOR, author of *Canoe Country: The Making of Canada*

"God bless Kevin Callan. The Happy Camper is still out there doing his thing and encouraging the rest of us to do the same. Still not entirely sure about the Kevin-and-Andy-La-Cage-aux-Folles-meets-the-Odd-Couple-or-a-pair-of-old-sneakers schtick but Callan charm comes in many forms. *Once Around Algonquin* is funny, corny, engaging and authentic with a dabbling of trail wisdom and life lessons woven into the tale of yet another epic canoe trip. Two blistered thumbs up!"
JAMES RAFFAN, author of *Circling the Midnight Sun, Deep Waters*, and many others.

"Kevin Callan is one of Canada's best-known paddlers, and few people know Algonquin Park like he does. *Once Around Algonquin* is at once a vivid account of a legendarily tough canoe trip, an illuminating history of one of Canada's best-loved wilderness areas, and a heartfelt plea for the park's ongoing protection. A must-read for canoe trippers everywhere."
ALEC ROSS, author of *Coke Stop in Emo: Adventures of a Long-Distance Paddler*

"Kevin Callan's *Once Around Algonquin* is an exciting tale of misadventure on the toughest route in Ontario's most well-loved wilderness. Enjoy history of Algonquin's paddling paradise while you chuckle along with the tales behind the blisters and bruises in this bromance adventure tale, all told with Callan's trademark humor."
KAYDI PYETTE, editor, *Paddling Magazine*

www.ingramcontent.com/pod-product-compliance
Lightning Source LLC
Chambersburg PA
CBHW030525080526
44586CB00011B/327